I0024303

Noah Brooks

The Fairport Nine

Noah Brooks

The Fairport Nine

ISBN/EAN: 9783742897893

Manufactured in Europe, USA, Canada, Australia, Japa

Cover: Foto ©Thomas Meinert / pixelio.de

Manufactured and distributed by brebook publishing software
(www.brebook.com)

Noah Brooks

The Fairport Nine

THE

FAIRPORT NINE

BY

NOAH BROOKS

AUTHOR OF "THE BOY EMIGRANTS" ETC.

NEW YORK
CHARLES SCRIBNER'S SONS

CONTENTS.

THE FAIRPORT NINE.

CHAPTER I.

RINGING THE BELL.

IN Fairport, every boy slept with some other boy on the night before the Fourth of July. If any boy did sleep in his own bed, it was because he had a playmate with him. But, for the most part, the boys of that period thought it poor fun to sleep at home on that eventful night. They all preferred to sleep in barns, hay-mows, or some other out-of-the-way and unusual place. It was a sign that a fellow was a milk-sop if he slept in a real bed on that night, except under such circumstances as have just been referred to. For there was a great deal to be done on the night before the Fourth. In the first place, there was a bonfire to be built on the common. There was a large, bare spot in the middle of the common where the grass refused to grow

1

from one year's end to another, because the bonfire was built there on the night before the Fourth. And to feed that fire, it was necessary to gather much fuel from various and distant places. Spare barrels, store-boxes, and occasionally a loose board from off some careless person's fence were to be brought in. The boys did not take gates off their hinges to kindle the fire, as tradition said that their older brothers did, when they were. boys. The time of which I write was a great improvement on that elder period. No boy fed the bonfire with anything more valuable than the few loose things that could be picked up without alarming the neighbors. The neighbors were easily alarmed, anyhow. There was a class of old ladies in Fairport who never remembered from one Fourth of July to another that, on the night before it, the boys, ever since there were any boys, built a bonfire on the common. So, when the bright flames began to rise up in the darkness, one or more of these timid women would be sure to come out on her door-step and cry: "Boys! Boys! What are you doing? You'll set the town a-fire, you pesky boys!"

Jo Murch (his whole name was Jotham Aug tus Murch) used to be very much mortified wl his mother came out like that, and he would sa "Now, Ma, don't be so foolish. There isn't a danger of our setting anything a-fire!" On one of the Selectmen of the town, a very dignified and truly awful person, came upon the common to see what the boys were at. It was nearly midnight, and it seemed as if something alarming was about to happen when the great man came out at that time of night. But he only looked the party of boys all over, as if to be sure that he would know them again, if anything happened, and then he went away, telling them to be careful of the sparks.

"My! Wasn't I afraid he would see old Snelgro's wheelbarrow!" said Ned Martin, when the Selectman was gone.

At midnight, as near as they could guess, it was necessary that the meeting-house bell should be rung. At least, every Fairport boy thought it was necessary; and it was rung. There was a bell on the school-house at the right of the common, only, as nobody but the nearest neighbors objected to the ringing of this bell, the boys did not much enjoy ringing it. They took a pull at it, once in a while, for fear that the folks around would not know t the glorious Fourth had arrived. The folks ally found it out before day-break. The town l was on the Unitarian meeting-house, below the ool-house, and facing the street which skirted bottom of the common. To ring this bell was only necessary, but it was also a great feat. e Selectmen had forbidden that the bell should be rung by anybody but the town sexton, except in case of fire. From time immemorial, Old Fitts had been the town sexton, and if any man really hated boys, Old Fitts did. Probably he never was a boy. It seemed absurd to think that he ever could have been a boy. Boys were his natural enemies. They used to shin up the lightning-rod of the church and catch the pigeons which he reared in the belfry ; and they used to ring the bell on the night before the Fourth of July. Generation after generation of boys had done this ; but, somehow, Old Fitts could never become reconciled to it. On the particular night about which I am going to write, Old Fitts had not only nailed up one of the two church doors and put an extra padlock on the other, but he had carried away the bell-rope. The Fairport boys were a curious set. They laughed among themselves when they saw him going home, after he had rung the nine o'clock bell, with the long bell-rope coiled up on his back. But when they flew to the doors, after he was well out of sight, and beheld the defenses which he had put on them, they began to think that, for the first time in the history of the world, the bell would not be rung on the night before the Fourth of July.

As the boys scattered to the barns and hay-mows where they had chosen to sleep, Ned Martin said to his crony, Sam Perkins :

"I 'll ring that bell before daylight, you see."

" But how, Ned ? "

Now, Sam was the leader of the boys in almost all of the mischief that was afoot, and he was, beside all that, the captain of the Fairport Nine. For Fairport had a base-ball nine, and it was the terror of the surrounding villages. Of course, Sam did not want any other boy to lead off in a feat of this kind unless he had a hand in it himself. But Ned Martin knew a thing or two, and Sam was sure that he would ring the bell, if he said so. And when the boys, three of them, for Hi Hatch bunked in with them that night, were safely hidden in the hay, Ned unfolded to them his plan. It was a good scheme, and all agreed to it.

In all the world, probably, there is no stillness like that which comes between nine o'clock and the time when the Fairport boys get up to ring the bell and build their bonfire, on the night before the Fourth of July. At least, Hiram Hatch thought so that night, as he lay awake in the hay in his father's barn, listening to the heavy breathing of his mates. The spears of hay tickled his ear so that he could not get to sleep ; and the stillness was awful. He almost wished that he was snug in his own bed, and he wondered why Ned and Sam should go to sleep so soon, and he should be so broad awake. There was a sound of something on the barn floor below.

I† ⁣d ! Then he heard a ghostly whisper, the hair rising on his head. Desperately ⁣ng Sam in the back he whispered :

" There is something climbing up the ladder ! "

Sam bounced up and cried : " What's—what's that ! "

There was a scrambling and a rush of feet below, and all was still again. But Hiram was too badly scared to go to sleep at once, and when, tired out by his long vigil, he did drop off into slumber, he slept so soundly that Sam had hard work to wake him, as he shook him and shouted in his ear :

" Remember you have got to play second base, to-day."

" What do you s'pose that was in the barn, just now ? " shivered Hiram, for the midnights in Fairport are cool, seeing that the town is on Penobscot Bay, on the cold coast of Maine.

" Oh bother ! " said Sam. " Let's get out of this as still as we can. If your father should hear us, as likely as not he 'd fire that double-barrelled shot-gun at us."

Hiram held his peace, for the double-barrelled shot-gun was a sore subject with him, since he had promised to carry it off on the sly and have it for firing the usual midnight salute. He was comforted now by the reflection that he had not the responsibility of that gun on his mind ; and Ned assured

him that the noise in the night was probably only
made by some of the other boys who had intended
to steal a place to sleep, without waking up the
rightful tenants.

Silently, and as if bent on some dreadful deed,
dark forms now stole in from all around, and clustered in the middle of the common. A crockery
crate, filled with straw, and stuck all around with
pickets from some slothful man's dilapidated fence,
was set on fire. The cheerful blaze, ascending,
lighted up the fronts of the houses on the edge of
the common, and shed a lurid glare on the tall elms
which stood tremulously in the midnight air. The
flames warmed the boys, and revived their spirits,
somewhat damped by cold and lack of sleep.

"Hurrah for the Fourth of July!" shouted Bill
Watson, a burly little chap, the right fielder, and
better known as "Chunky." Then every other
fellow cried "Hurrah for the Fourth of July!"
And it was felt that the fun had begun.

Amidst great enthusiasm, Pat Adams now fired
off his gun. It was only a single-barrelled one, to
be sure, but it spoke well for itself. Pat's name was
James Patterson Adams, but he was known, for
short, as Pat Adams, and, when the boys were not
in much of a hurry, he was called Jim Pat Adams,
to distinguish him from another Jim whose name
was not Adams. When the bang of Pat's gun rent

the air, there was a sound of opening windows, and
the boys knew that angry looks were directed
toward them from some of the houses roundabout.
There was a wild hurrah when Sam Black, assisted
by Billy Hetherington, staggered up to the fire with
the better part of a tar-barrel, which they had
hidden away some days before. There is no aris-
tocracy among real boys, and it was an evidence
of this truth that Sam Black, who was the only
negro boy in Fairport, was a crony of Billy Hetherington, whose father was the county judge, and had
been to Congress. If any boy had a right to be
" stuck up " it was Billy, whose family held themselves very high in Fairport. But Billy never once
thought of such a thing. If he had, his mates would
have cut him at once, and he would have found
himself alone in the village of boys. It was curious
that the only black boy in the town should be Black
by name. So Sam, who was a great favorite with
his comrades, was usually called " Blackie," a term
which carried with it no idea of contempt. Blackie
was the best fellow of the boys of that generation,
and, moreover, he knew more of the habits of the
birds, beasts, fish, and all manner of living wild
things, than most of the naturalists who write thick
books about the animal kingdom. The times and
seasons when birds come and go, and when they
mate, and where they build their nests, as well as the

secret lairs of the small game of the w̲ ...ing in were all as familiar to Blackie as if he hau ...n... his in the wilderness, and not in a house on st. the harbor's edge. d

"Three cheers for the left fielder!" cried Jo Murch, as Blackie, his face shining with satisfaction and pride, helped Billy Hetherington heave the tar-barrel on the blazing pile. "And now, boys, for the bell," he added, for it was already past twelve, one of the boys having reconnoitred, through the kitchen window of a neighboring house, to ascertain the time of night.

Ned Martin looked around on the little group of lads in his superior way, and said :

"Which of you fellows is the best on shinning a lightning-rod?" There was a great laugh when John Hale stoutly answered : "I am!" for John was so big and lubberly that he was never called anything but the "lob." In Fairport, the 'long-shoremen call any craft which is clumsy and un-wieldy "lob-sided," meaning, perhaps, that it is lop-sided, a phrase which may be found in the dictionaries. If one but stuck out a fist at Johnny Hale he fell over. And when the schoolmaster tried to get him up on the tall stool where it was the custom for boys to be hoisted for punishment, the master and Johnny invariably came down in a heap together on the floor, the "lob" was so very

1*

the air, "and so very heavy. Nevertheless, the
the b," for all his awkwardness, was the champion
toweher in ' Fairport, and the envy of the White
Thears, the rival club from the south end of town.

The "lob" was rejected as the champion climber,
however, and little Sam Murch, Jo's brother, was
selected for the feat of shinning up the lightning-rod
of the church.

As an aid, in case of need, the volunteered services of Blackie were also promptly accepted, for
the Fairport Nine never did anything that was not
"ship-shape and Bristol fashion," or, otherwise,
according to rule and discipline.

Old Major Boffin's house stood so near the meeting-house that one could toss a biscuit from the roof
of one to the other ; and the Major's grandson,
Ike, was a member of the party, though not of
the famous " Nine." This was lucky ; and it was
also lucky that the roof of the Major's house was
nearly flat, and that it had at each of the angles of
said roof a big, square chimney, so big that two or
three boys might hide behind one of them without
fear of detection. And when it was remembered
that the roof of the Major's house could be reached
by a lightning-rod, much easier of ascent than that
on the meeting-house, it was evident that fortune
favored the brave when it was necessary for the
brave to ring the bell on the night before the Fourth

of July. The testy old Major, calmly sleeping in
his bed, could not have dreamed how much his
property was contributing to the celebration of the
glorious Fourth, when, in addition to all this, Ned
Martin, carefully stripping the sheets, shirts, and
pillow-cases from the clothes-line in the Major's
garden, took the line and making one end fast to
the ankle of little Murch, gave him a hoist, and told
him to " go it " up the lightning-rod of the meeting-
house.

The projection of the eaves of the building set
the rod out from the side of it a great way, and, as
the rod was jointed in two or three places, it sway-
ed fearfully while Sam laboriously shinned up it.
Now and again, he would be flung round and round
by the swinging rod, as he passed over the clank-
ing joints, the clatter of which threatened to bring
the choleric Major down upon them at any moment.

" Hold fast, little one," hoarsely whispered Captain Sam from below, for Sam, with his usual facil-
ity for taking command, had now assumed the
direction of things. " Hold fast, or Blackie will be
on your heels." And Blackie, dancing up and
down with impatience, was ready to make a spring
at the rod when little Murch should be out of his
way.

" Bully for Sam," half shouted Ned Martin, for

the little fellow had reached the edge o. the far projecting eaves, and was now struggling to get over
the most difficult part. The boys below held their
breath, for it was a perilous place. The lightning-
rod, after turning up the edge of the shingles, was
fastened to the roof by strong staples which held it
firmly down and afforded almost no hold to which
even a boy's small and hook-like fingers could cling.
But little Sam was "clear grit," as his brother
proudly remarked in a suppressed whisper, and
while the silent spectators below all looked up, with
their hearts in their mouths, he turned the edge of
the eaves and went picking his way up the roof,
hand over hand. It was now Blackie's turn to go
up, but Captain Sam interfered, and declared that if
both of the best climbers went up into the meeting-
house belfry, there would be nobody to shin up to
the roof of the Major's house and carry the rope
from the bell, when it was made fast. Half-a-dozen
boys volunteered to go up the Major's lightning-
rod, but Ike Boffin agreed to "hook in" by the
back door, steal up the stairs to the roof, and take
care of the rope when there.

"So, then, you are to have all the fun of ringing
the bell, are you?" demanded Captain Sam, sarcastically.

"Well," said Ike, "you pick out four other
fellows, and I will undertake to get them up on our

roof, if they will promise to be mighty still about it."

Accordingly, Captain Sam, Ned Martin, Hi Hatch and Chunky were chosen to go up on the Major's roof, guided by Ike, who, with a quaking heart, opened the back door and let in these midnight conspirators. No cat could have climbed the stairs more softly than the five boys, Ike at the head. Barefoot and breathless, they stole by the door of the sacred chamber where the old Major, snoring manfully, was sleeping in happy unconsciousness of what was going on around him. Drawing a long breath, the five boys found themselves out on the roof at last. To their great delight and relief, they saw little Murch just shinning up the part of the rod which led from the roof to the belfry, not a very difficult job, in comparison with that which he had just finished. In a moment more he was in the belfry, and pausing on the balustrade which decorated the rim, he gave a noiseless cheer, dropped over to the inner side, and made fast to the clapper of the bell the end of the line which he had brought up with him. Ned Martin now dropped down from the roof of the Major's house one end of a mackerel line which he had with him. To this the boys below fastened the end of the line from the bell-clapper, and it was drawn up to Captain Sam, who took it up behind his chimney with great joy.

The boys on the ground now scattered to all parts of the common, at a whispered command from Captain Sam, and then the big bell struck a peal of mighty strokes, pulled by the sinewy hand of Sam. The night air quivered with the blows on the bell. Old Fitts' pigeons, affrighted by the midnight booming of the bell, flew out in crowds, scaring Sam Murch as they dashed in his face. The brave little lad swung himself over the balustrade, and, sliding down the roof in a hurry, was soon on the long and swaying rod below, and on firm ground once more, and then safe among his comrades.

"Those pesky boys," sighed Grandmother Boffin, as she turned uneasily in her sleep, but awake enough to know what was the cause of the horrible din which rent the air. The Major got out of bed, and, putting his head out of the window, addressed the darkness, commanding all in sound of his voice to disperse and go home, or take the consequences. But the old Major never forgot that he had been a boy once himself, although that was a great many years ago ; and when he went back to bed, smiling grimly to himself as the bell answered his warning with a yet louder peal, he said : " Well, mother, boys will be boys, you know. There's no law ag'in ringing the meeting-house bell on the night before the Fourth." The Major, although a hot-tempered man, remembered that he had fought in " the last war "—that of 1812—and something was due, he thought, to the day we celebrate.

A sudden idea struck the good grandmother. She crept out of bed, stole to the bedroom of her grandson, passed her hand over the vacant bed, and then going back to her chamber-window, cried into the air, as the Major had done, "You, Ike, wherever you are, don't you dare to come into the house for your breakfast!" Ike, who was now taking his turn at the clothes-line, laughed to himself. He remembered that he had a share in a boiled ham, a basket of apples and a paper of crackers, stowed away in Hatch's barn, under the hay.

Suddenly there was an alarm of "Fitts! Fitts!" from the boys stationed on the court-house steps, from which post they could see all the way down Howe's lane, up which the old sexton must come to the defense of his precious bell. Fortunately for the boys, Fitts never stirred out of doors, no matter how light the night, without his lantern. And the rays from that familiar lantern, "like a lightning-bug," as Billy Hetherington declared, now bobbed along the ground as Fitts climbed the hilly lane.

Warned in time, not a boy was in sight when the old sexton, grumbling to himself, reached the top of the hill and went across the bottom of the common toward the meeting-house. The bell continued

to ring, much to the delight of the boys hidden behind the chimneys and stowed away in various
nooks and corners below.   With infinite trouble,
Old Fitts got the door open, and with many a hard
word for the boys, toiled up the long stairs which
led to the belfry.   "Now, then, Ned, give her a
good one," whispered Captain Sam, as the old sexton's lantern, shining through the belfry windows,
showed that he was almost up to the bell, and, sure
enough, as Fitts put his head out of the scuttle
which opened to the deck of the belfry, a tremendous and audacious peal boomed directly over his
head.

The old man walked all around the big bell.
Not a boy was to be seen.   The rope, he knew,
was safe in his own house, and there was no sign
of anything by which the bell could be rung.   The
light line leading to the roof of the Boffin house
was too small to be noticed as it lay on the slanting
deck of the belfry.   The boys chuckled to themselves as they watched the puzzled old man walking
around the bell, again and again peering over the
balustrade, as if to see if some small boy were cir-
cling around in the air with the scared pigeons which
silently flew about their master's head.   It was very
queer, so it was.

Just then, the "lob," who was never known to
stand up when he could fall down, slipped on the

roof behind the Boffin chimney that hid him. He
might have slid off to the ground below if he had
not put out his hand to save himself by grabbing
at the boy next to him, which happened to be Sam,
who tried to shake the "lob" from him. It was in
vain, and the two boys came down in a heap behind the chimney, Sam pulling the rope with him.
As he fell, the bell, of course, was given another
peal, and the rope in the belfry flew up before the
astonished eyes of the old sexton. Fitts stooped,
cut the line, and, shaking his fist in the direction
of the Major's house, cried, "I've stopped your
fun this time, you young varmints;" and so he
had. When he had carefully locked the scuttle of
the belfry, descended the stairs and gone home,
his light disappearing in the distance, the four boys
on the roof, somewhat crestfallen, silently slid down
the Major's lightning-rod, and made their way up
to the bonfire. The "lob" was overwhelmed with
ridicule for his share in the failure of the bell-
ringing feat. "And he wanted to shin up the
meeting-house lightning-rod!" said Captain Sam,
derisively.

Blackie, however, soon found a way to remedy .
the mischief. He went up the lightning-rod again
with the agility of a cat, spliced the line, then, dis-
daining to go up through the Major's house, he
shinned up its lightning-rod and speedily had the

bell a-ringing merrily. Meantime, the boys about
the bonfire were doing their best to celebrate the
night by firing the few pieces of small arms which
they had ; and their fire-crackers were exploded—
sparingly, however, as it was borne in mind that
the Fourth was yet to come, and more noise would
be needed for the day.

Hiram Hatch, returning from a visit to the back
of Major Boffin's house to encourage Blackie, who
was pulling away lustily at the bell-rope, cast his
eyes on the fire, and, to his horror, spied the re-
mains of the leaching-tub which he knew ought to
be standing on his father's barn floor.   " Where did
that come from ? " he demanded.   Nobody knew,
but Chunky guessed that Jo Murch and George
Bridges had thrown it on the fire.

"That came out of my father's barn," said Hi,
stoutly, " and the fellow that took it is a mean
sneak, and I don't care who he is."

" I don't see that it is any meaner to take that
leaching-tub out of Deacon Hatch's barn than it is
to steal old Boffin's clothes-line, or Judge Nelson's
chicken-coop, so there," said Jo Murch.

As the Judge's coop had been ravished by Hiram,
he felt condemned ; but he replied, hotly, that
there was a big difference between taking an old
chicken-coop, only fit for kindlings, anyhow, and
stealing a leaching-tub out of a man's barn.   Then,

suddenly remembering the mysterious noises which he had heard while he was trying to go to sleep, he exclaimed, with his small fist before Jo Murch's nose, "And you came in there and stole that tub while we were in the hay-loft. I heard you."

"Yes, and mighty scared you were, too," Jo replied, with an unpleasant sneer.

There were symptoms of a fight, when one of the sentries on the court-house steps shouted "Fitts! Fitts!" Then all the boys, in their anxiety for the bell, scattered to points about the meeting-house from which they could see the fate of Blackie, who, perceiving the lantern of the old sexton coming, improved the time by giving the bell as many and as vigorous strokes as possible.

Grumbling and groaning to himself, the sexton slowly climbed the belfry stairs once more, and was soon on the upper deck. "Why, oh why, didn't I nail down that scuttle?" groaned little Blackie, as, from behind his chimney, he saw the old man emerge upon the belfry deck. Blackie consoled himself with the reflection that he would do this the next time the coast was clear. But he was doomed to disappointment. Fitts, as soon as he had cut the line, for the second time, gave it a strong pull, and a sudden pull, and poor Blackie, not for a moment dreaming what was going to happen, was jerked out from behind the chimney, and, still hold-

ing on, across the scuttle, which had been left
open.

"Aha! It's you, is it; you, you black limb, is
it?" cried Old Fitts, exultingly, as the boy came
dimly into sight from behind the chimney. "Major
Boffin! There's a burglar on your roof!" shouted
the old man, as he tugged at the line which Blackie
sturdily refused to let go.

"Shame! Shame! Old Fitts!" shrieked several
of the boys below, in their concealment. "He's
no burglar, and you know it."

In the midst of the racket, Major Boffin, with a
grim smile on his face, put his head out of the window, and, after shouting "Thieves! Thieves!"
at the top of his voice, fired into the sky a horse-
pistol which he kept loaded for the entertainment
of the midnight cats that sometimes disturbed his
slumbers. A profound silence followed this volley.
Even Old Fitts was quiet in his belfry; and Blackie,
taking advantage of the lull, dropped the line which
he had held, and softly crept down the roof, clutched
the lightning-rod, slid to the ground, and made off
in the darkness.

"If I catch those pesky boys around here again
to-night," said the angry sexton, "I'll put a load
of buckshot into some of 'em."

"Never you fear," answered the Major, "you
will never catch them. Sooner catch a lot of

weasels." And the old man shut down his window with a bang.

Fitts descended into the little loft below the belfry, and, though the boys waited for his appearance beneath, his lantern did not shed its beams again on the outside of the meeting-house.

"He's camping in the steeple!" cried the boys, in alarm. And so he was. Determined to stop the ringing of the bell, and afraid to leave his post of duty, the old man lay down on the floor of the loft, secure in the knowledge that no enemy could scale the roof without awakening him. The boys gathered in a knot below, examined the ground and confessed that, for once, they were circumvented.

It was growing toward morning. The east was pale with the first streaks of dawn. It had been a tiresome night. The great base-ball match was coming off on that day. The bell had been rung. The Nine went to bed, and Fairport was quiet at last.

CHAPTER II.

THE GREAT MATCH.

BETWEEN the White Bears and the Fairport Nine there was, in the opinion of the older people, a great gulf fixed. The White Bears were, for the most part, the sons of fishermen, 'longshoremen, and men who, in the expressive language of the place, "did chores" about town. This was the social gulf which separated the famous Nine and the White Bears. Then the boys who called themselves White Bears were noted for their rough mischief. If an unfortunate cow was found with her tail cut off, it was the work of a White Bear. And when the old revolutionary cannon which had stood for years, with its breech in the ground, an upright landmark, on the corner of Main street, was dug up and pitched off the end of Adams's wharf, everybody knew that the White Bears had been out on an errand of malicious mischief. The boys of Fairport, who were represented by the famous Nine, were not goody-goody youngsters ; indeed, some of the

older folks thought that they ought to be a great
deal better than they were, but they were never
accused of being ruffianly or cruel, or destructive ;
and all these traits were justly set down to the
credit of the White Bears. Besides all this, the
White Bears lived in the scattered and dingy groups
of houses at the south end of the village ; and this,
until they took for themselves the name by which
they were better known, gave them the title of the
Southenders. To be a Southender was to be a
rough fellow, with small respect for law, order, or
the rights of others.

The White Bears, with all their muscle, were not
very much better in the base-ball field than the
Fairport Nine. They were trained, many of them,
in the cod fishing fleet, which used to sail to the
Grand Banks, before the fishing business went into
the hands of our Canadian neighbors. And, ex-
posed as they all were to the hard life and rough
usage of those who pick up a scanty living on the
coast of Maine, they were as tough and rugged as
the polar bear, whose name they took in a spirit of
boasting and bravado. Sam Booden was their captain, and he was the roughest and the toughest of
the gang. Sam had regularly " walloped " the
village schoolmaster, as fast as a new one came to
town ; and, as he was as regularly turned out of
school, his education was none of the best. He

never stayed in school any longer than to have his first chance at the master, and, as boys of his class were not often at home during the summer, his acquaintance with the inside of a school-house was very limited.

But Sam was at home long enough to make a tolerable base-ball player, and at the third base he was perhaps the very best in all Fairport. Jake Coombs was the pitcher of the White Bears, and a first-rate pitcher he was. He had been two voyages as cook on a mackerelling schooner, and was probably the most quarrelsome boy in Fairport. Usually, he had a black eye, the mark of one of his latest fights. Of course, all of his fingers were more or less out of shape. But that is the proper badge of an accomplished base-ball player. Eph Weeks was the catcher of the White Bears, and Joe Patchen was the first base. George Bridges, their second base, was the decentest boy of the gang. He was in full fellowship with the Fairport Nine, and, although he was sometimes obliged to do dirty work at hog-killing time (for his father was the town butcher) about the houses of some of the more favored boys of the place, he was a crony and a companion to many of the favorite Nine.

As I have said, Sam Booden was the third base, as well as captain of the White Bears. Eph Mullett was their short stop, and as Eph had an unfortunate defect in his speech which made his words seem to come from his nose rather than his mouth, he was usually known as " Nosey " among the boys of Fairport. In summer time he wore a parti-colored tunic, or cooler, from which circumstance he was sometimes called " The Turkey," or " Turk," as it suited the fancy of his dear friends and associates. With Dan Morey in the left field, Joe Fitts in centre field, and Peletiah Snelgro in right field, the Nine of the White Bears is complete.

Whenever Sam Perkins met one of the White Bears, he was wont to say, as if addressing the universe :

" The Fairport Nine is the Nine that I belong to, and I am not ashamed to own it either."

No White Bear ever dared to take that up, as the saying is, and as Sam never had the luck to encounter more than one of the Bears when he was alone, he was always safe in his defiance. But Sam was deeply mortified when his Nine played what he called a scrub game with the White Bears, and were consequently defeated with great disgrace. For this defeat, Sam always blamed Jo Murch, who was playing centre field that day, and not at first base where he usually belonged. On that momentous occasion, he made a muff of a high fly ball, far out in the left centre, in the eighth inning, which allowed the White Bears to score three runs. To

tell the whole truth, the White Bears were considered the worst enemies of the Fairports on the base-
ball field, as they had defeated all the other clubs in
the small towns roundabout, and had held the championship for the last two seasons, but were hard-
pressed for this particular season by the White
Bears. This was the reason why this game on the
Fourth of July was so important. It was to decide
the championship of Fairport, and of North Fairport, Penobscot, and Riversville.

Now, every boy knows why Sam Perkins was
anxious when he tumbled out of bed on Fourth of
July morning, at the call of his mother. Had he
been left to himself, he would have slept until noon.
A boy who has got up at midnight, and has gone
to bed again at daylight, might be reasonably
sleepy at so early an hour as seven o'clock. But
hard work was to be done.

The White Bears had beaten the Fairports in the
latest, or second, game for championship, it is
true, but the first game of the series was won by the
Fairports by a score of eight to one, a tremendous
victory, to be sure. Now had come the momentous day when the third and decisive game was to
be played. And when Sam looked anxiously at
the sky, he was troubled to notice that a dark cloud
hung low down in the West, just over the old fort
in which the match was to be played.

"Just our luck," he grumbled, when .
trusty lieutenant, Ned Martin, on the common,
where he was hunting around in the ashes of last
night's fire for a lost jack-knife. "Just our luck!
I 'll bet it rains to-day and spoils all our fun. Our
fellows are all in first-rate shape. No sprained
legs, no broken fingers, and here it comes up to
rain, as sure as a gun. It 's too bad, so it is."

"Oh, never mind," said the more cheerful Ned.
"If it rains, the Bears will be as badly off as we
are ; that 's one comfort ; wont they? "

"But we want to have this thing over with,"
replied Sam. "The Bears have been poking that
last game at us ever since they beat us. But they
sha'n't have a chance to crow over us after to-day,
as sure as my name is Perkins," he added, more
hopefully. "I 'll play my position at short stop for
all it is worth, you just be sure of that now, Neddy,
my boy," and Captain Sam Perkins stretched himself, with a tremendous yawn, wishing that he had
had a good night's rest by way of preparation for
the day's work.

Fairport is built on the sunny side of a peninsula
which juts out into Penobscot Bay. To the north
and west, the land slopes sharply down to a little
cove, known to the youth of the village as "the
Back Cove." To the east and south, the land falls
off more gradually to the harbor's edge, and on

the gently falling slope is nestled the old town
shaded with elms, horse-chestnuts and maples.

On the ridge which forms the backbone of the
promontory is the old fort, a huge, high earthwork, inclosing about three acres of ground, and
built by the British troops in the war of the Revolution.

Once there was a brick barrack in the fort, and in
one corner is still shown the entrance to a dungeon
dug into the thick mass of earth, stone and timber
which forms the fort. The barrack has disappeared, and the inclosed space is as smooth and level as
a ball-ground should be. Laying off the field
against one of the angles of the earthwork, they had
a grassy field under foot, while the slopes of the
fort furnished seating-places for the spectators, as
well as a screen for the catcher. It is not likely
that the British commander, General McLean,
when he built this fort, in 1779, and called it Fort
George, after his royal master, George III., of
England, ever thought what a service he was doing for the boys of Fairport. But it is true that no
base-ball field in this or any other country can be
compared with that which the British army left for
generations of boys at Fairport. And when, on
the memorable Fourth of July, the Fairport Nine
met the White Bears for the fight for the championship, the old fort presented a brilliant sight.

On the grassy slopes of the ramparts, commanding a good view of the field, were all the nice girls of the village, some of whom had concealed about them the gay rosettes, made of the Nine's cherry-colored ribbon, with which each purposed to decorate a certain favorite player, in case all went well with the Nine of Fairport. The boys who were not of the Nine, but who hoped to be, some day, were scattered about among the bright groups on the slopes, or crowded together just outside of the limits of the field. It was a pretty sight and a momentous day.

Captain Samuel Perkins placed his men thus: Pitcher—Ned Martin; catcher—the "lob"; first base—Jo Murch; second base—Hi Hatch; third base—Pat Adams; short stop—Sam Perkins; left field—Samuel Black, colored member, and better known as "Blackie"; centre field—Billy Hetherington; right field—Bill Watson, otherwise known as "Chunky." The captain surveyed his team with mingled pride and anxiety, looked at the sky, which was dark with clouds, and then calmly tossed up the copper with the Captain of the White Bears, Samuel Booden, to decide which should go first to the bat. The toss was won by the proud captain of the Fairport Nine, who yelled, "We'll take the field!"

They always thought it an advantage to go first

to the field, and as the White Bears took up the
bat, a smile of satisfaction ran over the faces of the
illustrious Nine of Fairport. The Bears did not find
it very easy to hit the skilful pitching of Ned Martin ; and Semantha Sellers, sitting on the grassy
rampart beside Mary Ann Martin, said, with a
chuckle of delight, " I s'pose Pel Snelgro thinks
he can play ball, but just see him whang the air
every time Ned fires that ball. Ned has got the
curve down fine, has n't he, Mary Ann ? "

" Do hush and look at that catch," for at that
moment Peletiah Snelgro sent a hot liner to Pat
Adams, at third base. Pat made an extraordinary
catch, taking it with one hand, and with a light
spring in the air, which won him a round of applause from the girls sitting on the slopes of the
fort ; and even the boy spectators, outside of the
field, murmured their approbation. Pat took off
his cap and bowed low to the ladies in reply to this
compliment. Jake Coombs was the next striker
for the Bears, and he sent a foul tip behind the bat
which struck the " lob," catcher for the Fairports,
square on the nose. The " lob " doubled himself
up in pain, and a perceptible shudder ran through
the sympathizing crowd of girls on the rampart.
" What a shame ! " cried Phœbe Noyes, who had
a tender heart, and admired very much the rosy
face and blue eyes of the " lob." But John stout-

ly declared that it was " nothing," although the blood dropped freely from his inflamed pug-nose. Cold water was brought from the spring, half of the boys of Fairport volunteering to sop the "lob's" face, and run a cold iron spoon down his back, or hold his nose at the bridge, or do any of those things which any bright boy knows are sovereign remedies for the nose-bleed.

This diversion over, Captain Sam Booden went to the bat. "Now look out for squalls, you stuck-up Fairport Niners," said Nance Grindle, with withering sarcasm. Nance was a Southender, and was "second girl" in the family of the Hethering-tons, and cordially hated all aristocrats. Sure enough, Booden sent a daisy-cutter toward Hi Hatch, at second base, but Hi picked it up finely, and so Captain Sam Booden retired at first base, and the White Bears also retired without a score.

"A goose egg! A goose egg!" shouted the friends of the Fairport Nine. Captain Sam Perkins, too glad to speak, walked over to Hiram and wrung his hand in silence. It was now the first inning of the Fairports, and they did some very heavy batting, and scored five runs before their side was put out, three of them being home runs. But there were no special features of the game, and the girl-champions of the Fairports were not sorry when their friends were out once more. "They

do so much better in the field," they said, inno-
cently.

But the Fairport Nine had a decided lead, and
the chances were that they would have kept it to
the end and have won the game, but, just as the
White Bears were going to their second inning,
great drops of rain began to fall, and the storm
which Captain Sam had been dreading all day was
upon them. The girls put up their parasols and
umbrellas, and expressed their intention to stay and
see the game through, rain or shine. But the umpire, Mr. Sylvanus Tilden, of North Fairport,
called the game, which was accordingly postponed
until next day. " Just our luck ! " grumbled Captain Sam, as the Nine went down the hill into town.
It was a dismal ending of a Fourth which had begun so noisily, with the pealing of bells, the firing
of guns, and the flaming of bonfires, prophesied by
one of the revolutionary forefathers.

"Just our luck!" grumbled Sam, next day,
when he saw that the sky was cloudless, and that
the silvery waters of the bay reflected Nautilus Isl-
and, Gray's Head and Hainey's Point as if in a
looking-glass. "Some days it rains, and then,
again, some days it don't rain. Yesterday, just as
we were making ready to wallop the White Bears,
and had a lead of 5 to 0, it ups and rains, and so
puts a stop to the game. To-day not a wet cloud

shows its face in the sky. You look over the fort and you can see the whole of Brigadier's Island reflected in Penobscot Bay, just as if it was on the bottom of a new tin pan. Before this game is over, boys, you 'll wish a long shower would come and save the feelings of the bully Nine of Fairport ; now you see."

"Sam is always croaking," said Blackie, who was always looking on the bright side of things, as if his spirit was much lighter than his face. But when Sam lost the toss and the White Bears took the field and their opponents went to the bat first, things did look a little gloomy for the Fairports. And when their first inning was finished without scoring one run to their credit, even the calm and stolid "Iob" felt a sinking at the heart.

"It 's too bad," said pretty Alice Martin, shaking her yellow curls with emphasis. "It 's too bad for anything, and if I was Sam Perkins I 'd give that Coombs boy an awful whipping. Every time one of the White Bears' makes a base hit, he just grins like a chessy-cat, and makes up a face as if to say that he did it all. He 's perfectly horrid !"

But serious business was now in hand, for the Bears went to the bat in high spirits. It was the first time that they, or any other nine, had prevented the Fairports from making one run. They had a right to feel pleased. "Mightily tickled,"

2*

Sarah Judkins confidentially said they were, when
she leaned over and whispered her opinion into
Phœbe Noyes's sun-bonnet.

Before the Fairports went to their places, Captain Sam went among his forces and warned them
that the White Bears were playing at their very
best that day, and that if they would win it must
be with hard work, cool heads, and, above all, no
nonsense.   The game went on rapidly to the close
of the eighth inning, and, up to that time, the Fairport Nine had not been able to make a single run,
and their score stood exactly where it did at the
close of their first inning of the day before.   The
White Bears, however, crept up, making a run at a
time, until, when their opponents went to the bat
on the eighth, and the Fairport's last inning, the
score stood 5 to 5.   Sam Perkins was the first
striker, and while he was selecting his bat, his comrades noticed, with some surprise, that the White
Bears had quietly changed their pitcher.   The redoubtable Eph Mullett, otherwise "Nosey," and
otherwise "Turkey," went to the place of pitcher,
and Jake Coombs took the left field, while Dan
Morey went to short stop, where "Nosey" had
been playing.   This move did not disconcert Sam
in the least.   He was one of the strongest hitters
of his Nine, and was almost always safe.

There was not a sound.   Even the chattering

young ladies on the slopes of the rampart were as quiet as so many mice. They watched the game with the most intense interest, and, as for their friends in the Nine, they did not dare to speak, and hardly to breathe, for fear they might lose some point in the style of the new pitcher. Then came the umpire's question : " Where will you have the ball ? "

"Knee high," was Sam's steady reply, which could be heard by every person inside of the fort. Eph Mullett delivered the ball ; it went like lightning. Sam did not even make a motion to strike at it, and his fellows, who were waiting their turn on the bench near by, looked at each other in speechless amazement. But the gallant captain hit the next ball and sent it whizzing along the ground, and made the first base. Cheery little Blackie was next at the bat. "See the darkey!" scoffed Nance Grindle. "Thinks he is as good as a white man, don't he? So stuck-up along with Billy Hetherington! Sakes alive! What 's he at, anyhow?" For Blackie made two attempts to hit the ball delivered by Mullett, and in vain.

Meantime, however, Sam Perkins had stolen to his second base, and Blackie, with a mighty effort, gave him his third base by a masterly stroke that sent the ball to centre field. Now it was Ned Martin's turn to distinguish himself. With two players on the bases, it required very delicate playing. Ned played cautiously until he got a ball that almost everybody thought would bring home the two men on the bases. Alas! it went straight into the hands of the first base, who returned it with surprising dexterity to the catcher at home base, just in time to put out Sam Perkins by a hair's-breadth.

A double play for the "White Bears," two out on the side of the "Fairports," and not a run scored,—this prospect was not bright for the famous Nine. Fleet-footed Blackie was at second base, however, and Billy Hetherington, next to Sam Perkins, the best striker of the Fairport Nine, was the next man at the bat. Billy was tall and lank, for his years, and was sometimes called "Crane," by way of joke. But he had an unerring eye, and was as cool as a cucumber under any and all circumstances. Billy struck the first ball, and Blackie was off like a deer for third base. But, contrary to all expectations, Billy's ball was a foul, and, fortunately, as it turned out, went away out of the catcher's reach, among the thistles which grew at the base of the bastion. And so Blackie had time to resume his position at second base once more. Billy's next hit was a high-flyer, and as his comrades saw the centre fielder move back to get in range of the descending ball, their hearts almost stood still. They saw the ball go right through his hands, and then they breathed a long sigh of relief which was echoed among the very nicest girls on the side of the fort. Sam Perkins treated the spectators to a few steps of his favorite war-dance.

But the joy of the Fairports was short-lived. The "lob," their next batsman, sent a foul ball straight up over his head, and it fell plumb into the hands of the catcher. This ended the last inning of the Fairport Nine, and they had not made one run that day. Their only hope now was to "skunk" the White Bears, who were coming to the bat with their faces aglow with satisfaction and anticipated triumph. This, at least, might prolong the game, which could result in a tie.

When the Fairports went to the field in the ninth inning, it was evident that their spirits were a little drooping.

"I don't see our way out of this pickle," said Billy Hetherington to his sable chum, as they passed each other on their way to their respective stations.

"Keep a stiff upper lip, Billy," replied his hopeful crony. "I've seen sicker cats than this get well."

Billy thought to himself that, though a cat may have nine lives, the Fairport Nine did not have more than one chance in a thousand to beat the

White Bears in this match ; and then all would be
over.

The sympathies of the spectators were unmis-
takably with the Fairports, and when Pat Adams,
at third base, took a hot ball straight from Joe
Patchen's bat, with one hand, almost precisely as
he had done the day before, there was a breezy
ripple of applause all along the side of the fort
where the girls were the thickest in a group. Dan
Morey was their next striker. He sent a ball
straight over to little Blackie, at left field. Blackie
was watching the ball as it described a beautiful
ascending curve in the air, but his quick eye had
also marked the tall thistles on the top of the fort
nodding in the wind, which was now rising somewhat. He took a position a little to the right of
the place where everybody thought the ball should
fall. Captain Sam, at short stop, saw this and
ground his teeth with rage, and inwardly groaned
" he 'll make a muff!" But the colored member
of the Nine knew what he was about. The wind
took the ball a little to the north ; it then descended
with a rush, and dropped directly into his tawny
hands ; and good Blackie held it like a vice, doubling himself over in his anxiety to grip it. A scream
of delight went up from the rampart where the
girls waved their sun-bonnets with joy. The Fairports winked encouragingly at each other, and Cap-

tain Sam muttered an apology to Blackie, as he was in the habit of talking to himself. The White Bears had not made a run yet, and they had two players out. The prospect was decidedly better.

George Bridges was their next batsman, and he was always to be feared. As he stood in position, wearing his usual pleasant expression, but with a look of dogged determination on his brown face, everybody knew that he " meant business," as the Fairports were saying to themselves. If he once got a good blow at that ball, the chances were that it would go at a tremendous rate somewhere. Silently, Captain Sam motioned his fielders to fall back. The precaution was well taken. Bridges had a square hit at the ball, and sent it away over the head of Billy Hetherington at centre field. Before he could get it and throw it to Ned Martin, the pitcher, George Bridges had made his third base. Joe Fitts was the next man to stand up before the pitcher of the Fairports, and to him the White Bears now looked for success. He must hit the ball so as to bring George home, and if he could only do this, the game was won. It was a thrilling crisis. A hush fell on the field. The flower-bed of sun-bonnets and parasols on the rampart and the side of the fort ceased its fluttering in the wind and sunshine. Even the boy friends of the White Bears did not speak, although they showed

by their looks that they had confidence in Joe's
ability to do something great. And then Jemima
Pegg, a long-legged girl who worked in the lobster-
packing factory, stood up and waved her bonnet,
crying out, " Go it, Joe ! Now 's yer chance ! "

Joe struck at the ball twice, but missed it. At
the third attempt, however, he was more fortunate.
He sent it whizzing through the air over to Pat
Adams, at third base. Joe went for the first base,
as fast as his legs could carry him, George Bridges
did the same in the direction of the home base, and,
to the confusion and grief of the Fairports and their
fair friends, Pat Adams muffed that ball. " Oh,
Patsy ! Patsy ! How could you do so ? " groaned
Captain Sam. For that muff virtually lost the game,
and the crisis was past. But, before the White
Bears' third player was put out, the score-keepers
had to allow them a home run for Jake Coombs,
which, with Joe's one, made the score five to eight
in favor of the White Bears, and the next striker
was put out by a foul.

The great match was over, and pretty Alice Martin, rising from her seat on the turf, said : " It 's too
awfully mean for anything for those Southenders
to get the pennant. But it was just splendid."
Alice was always a little mixed in her ideas, but
she meant that the game was splendid. And so
thought and said a great many of the less personally

interested spectators, as they went down to ₂ of village. But so did not think Captain Sam when he saw the umpire hand the pennant over to the triumphant Booden, of the White Bears. That hero took it with a grin, and, waving the little strip of red and white bunting over his head, bawled —" It 's not so big as the ' William and Sally's ' burgee, boys, but it 's our 'n."

Sam and his mates turned away in speechless rage, but bold little Blackie called after the departing victors—" You had to work for it harder than you ever did before the mast ! So, now ! "

" Hush up, Blackie," said Billy Hetherington. " They 've won the championship, and the great match is over."

CHAPTER III.

THE HOUSE ON STILTS.

THE Black family lived in one of the houses on stilts. There was no good reason why there should have been any houses on stilts in Fairport. There was land enough everywhere to furnish room for the building of houses on the solid ground; yet, here, at the edge of the harbor and overhanging a steep bank, supported by tall, upright timbers, just like stilts, were built four houses. They were the delight of boys who were so unfortunate as to live in less picturesque dwellings. From the rear windows one could drop a fishing-line directly into the water, at high tide, and from these windows the tenants were accustomed to throw all the refuse and slops which less favorably situated people were obliged to carry out of doors. Then, too, from these same windows the boys who lived within could, at low tide, drop a handful of stones, or a bucket of water, on the head of the casual passenger beneath. Such advantages as these were fully appreciated by the boys of Fairport, every one of whom envied Sam Black the extraordinary facilities for fun which he had in one of the houses on stilts.

In the house at the end of the row, next to the path which led down to the shore from the village street, dwelt the father and mother of Sam Black. Nobody knew the real name of the paternal Black. It is not likely that he knew it himself. When he was a young lad, he had been stolen from the coast of Africa and sold into slavery in Brazil. Employed about the coffee warehouses of Rio de Janeiro, he managed to conceal himself on board of a Fairport brig loading there, and so was brought to Maine, where he found a wife on Plum Island, in the person of Thankful Snow, then the only colored woman in those parts. The fugitive slave from Brazil was known as Tumble Black, nobody knew why, but it is likely that his queer first name was a faint echo of his African name. In his life of slavery he was only known as Mumbo, a name which was so hateful that he dropped it as soon as he was a free man. The one only child of Tumble and Thankful Black was Sam, originally named Samuel Peleg Black, thus bearing, as a token of his father's gratitude, the names of the first and second mates of the brig "Draco," in which craft Tumble made his escape from South American slavery.

The houses on stilts were inhabited by the families of men who followed the sea as foremast hands, or who were the clam-diggers, wood-sawyers and wharf-keepers of the port. Tumble Black was whitewasher, wood-sawyer, and musician. In the Fairport Guards' Band, consisting of bass-drum and fife, Tumble played the fife; and very well he played it, too. He likewise played a French horn, chiefly for his own amusement. And on calm and still nights, when the moon was at her full, people on the water, gliding up the harbor, sometimes rested on their oars to listen to the melancholy notes of Tumble's horn as they floated over the bay from the window where he usually sat and poured out his soul in plaintive strains. A lady from Boston once said she thought that he was playing a lament for the lost land and home of his youth on Afric's coral strand.

Old Tumble was a prime favorite with the boys. He not only knew all the things about the sea, and shore, and the woods, which a boy admires in anybody, but he was full of strange and mysterious information about charms and witchcraft. It was said and believed that he could charm a bird from off a tree by a wild and peculiar whistle which he produced by making a sort of pipe of his thick lips. And it was notorious that he could bring the fish out of the sea by a motion of his hand. If this was

not so, how else could any one account for his
derful luck in fishing at times when nobody but
could catch anything? When the fishermen of the
port came in, empty-handed and discouraged, old
Tumble would put out in the bay for a little while,
alone, and come back in the nightfall with a great
haul of cod, haddock and hake. The fishermen
shook their heads, and, glancing up at the house on
stilts, would say that it " war n't for no good that
old Tumble-bug has been singing to himself out on
the bay, after dark."

The old man was full of story and anecdote about
his youthful life in Africa. He lived, he said, near
a great river which was called Quorra, and when
some of the boys looked into the map of Africa and
found that this was the native name of the Niger,
they felt as if they had discovered the river for
themselves. Old Tumble, also, delighted his small
hearers with scraps of the dialect which was his
native language. He had well-nigh forgotten the
words which he had used when he was a youngster
in his own land, so overlaid were they with Spanish, Portuguese and English ; but the boys of Fairport were delighted to talk enough Congo to mystify
the older people.

To ask for bread as " bomba," and for water as
" slee," or to say that they were " gaigai " when
they were hungry, was very great fun for these

young linguists. Sam, it should be added, did not
seem to take kindly to these little reminiscences of
his father's past life. His own language was as pure
as that of any of his playfellows, who, I am sorry to
say, used more slang than Sam did. But, as has
been intimated, Sam had all of his father's knowledge of the secrets of the sea and the wilderness.
He was never thought to be able to charm the fish
or the birds, but he was on more friendly terms
with these shy creatures than any other boy in Fairport.

Old Tumble, too, had the reputation of being
what was called "a money-digger;" not that he
actually spent his time, or any part of it, in digging
for money, but it was supposed that he could tell,
if he chose, how and where to dig for buried treasure. Fairport was full of stories and traditions of
buried pots and chests of money—the spoils of free-
booters and buccaneers who once sailed the seas,
and who put in to these lonely harbors to hide in
the earth their ill-gotten gains. It was believed by
many people that there was a magic by which hidden treasure could be found, if only one knew how
to use the magic. There were charms, divining-
rods, and various species of witchcraft, all more or
less requiring the aid of necromancy, by which
money hidden in the ground, or in the sea, could
be discovered. It was always necessary that such

a search should be made in the darkest of the night, when no moon was shining, when the tide was out, and when the planets in the heavens were in a peculiar position as to the fixed stars. Nobody knew just how all these signs were to be observed, but if any man did know, it was supposed that old Tumble was that man. He was black; he had been born in a land where magic, necromancy and the black art were understood, if anywhere. So, by general consent, it was agreed that if old Mr. Black chose to tell, he could guide anybody to hidden treasures of Captain Kidd and the rest of the bold buccaneers who hid their money in the earth and never came back for it. Nobody seemed to think that if old Tumble, who had had a hard time in the world because of his poverty, could find the lost treasures for others, he could find them for himself; and yet he had never been lucky enough to find anything more valuable than an old copper plate, bearing a Latin inscription, and supposed to be a relic of the French Jesuit mission, established here in the seventeenth century, when the Sieur D'Aulney ruled this land under General Razillai.

Billy Hetherington, sitting in the sunny kitchen of the house on stilts and looking over the bay, often wondered if old Tumble could really raise ghosts and spirits, as the gossips said he could. But he never mustered up the courage to ask him,

nor even to ask his crony, Sam, for he saw that such
a question would not please the boy, who had none
of the superstitions of the ignorant 'longshoremen
and toilers of the sea.   Once, taken off his guard by
his strong imagination, Billy, seeing Sam's father
put an odd-looking frying-pan on the fire, asked :
" Is that your storm-pan ? "   This was an unfortunate question.   There was a foolish belief among
the sailors of the bay that old Tumble had a pan by
which he could raise a storm at any time, by merely putting it on the fire ; and when Billy asked the
old man if that was the storm-pan, he put into words
the idle superstition which had led many a man,
when out in a gale at night to complain, " Old Tumble has got on his storm-pan."

Black looked angrily at the boy for a moment,
and Sam turned away his face, as if in reproach.
But the old man's features softened in an instant,
and he said, " No, my little gentleman, there is no
storm-pan ; at least, not that I know of, and they
are bad and wicked people who have filled your
head with such nonsense as that."

Billy felt reproved, and he was very much relieved when old Tumble took down his fife and played
for him an African melody, sad and wild, which,
he explained, had been taught him by his mother,
in their old home, years and years ago, and which
he had not forgotten and could not forget.   " Some-

times, when the fishermen hear this tune," he said, "they think that I am doing something to charm away the fish from the seine, or to bring on a spell of bad weather. If they knew how my poor old mother, dead and gone, I s'pose these many years, learned me this tune, they would laugh at themselves because they are so foolish."

Emboldened by the old man's burst of confidence, Billy had the courage to say "And they do say, Mr. Black, that you know how to dig for buried money, and how to find a spring of water that is hid in the ground."

"All nonsense, child, all nonsense. Nobody knows where to dig for hidden treasure, unless he has been told where it is. Anybody can dig if he knows *where* to dig."

"And can't you find springs of water? My father said you can."

"Yes, child, I can find a spring of water, providing the dew is off the grass, and it is airly morning, and my divining-rod is in tune." And here the old man took down a green wand of witch-hazel, forked at one end. Holding it with one prong in each hand, he added, "And when I walk over the ground, holding this upright, so, I can see it bend down whenever I pass over a spring hid in the ground. But the dew must be off of the grass, and the sun be up, but not up too high."

3

Sam was a little impatient at this, and he signed
to Billy to go out with him on the beach below.

" That is mighty curious, Sam, is'nt it ? " said
Billy, as he skipped a stone across the waves. " I
wish I had a divining-rod, I would find a spring
nearer our camp in the fort pasture. O ! say, Sam,"
he exclaimed, a bright idea striking him, " suppose
you get your father to go down back of the fort,
some day, when the dew is off the grass, and the sun
is not too high, and have him find a spring for us ;
it is so far to go for water to the gully from the
camp, every time we go a-Maying."

Sam dug his bare black toe thoughtfully in the
sand before he replied.

" Well, you see, Billy, I don't think that your
mother would like to have any such doings, for she
is awful particular, you know, about 'stitions and
things. Don't you remember how mad she was at
you and me for listening to old Ma'am Heath's
stuff about digging for money in the full of the
moon, down behind the block-house ? "

This was a sore point with Billy, for he had been
seriously reasoned with by his mother when he had
come home, full of a new project for money-digging,
in which he and Sam were to be aided by Vene
Snowman, a step-son of Ma'am Heath, the village
seeress. They were to find a toad with seven warts
on his back, a field-sparrow with seven white feathers

in his tail, and procure a crooked four-pence-ha'-penny, and seven tallow candles, and several other things, and Vene, whose full name was Sylvanus, was to be prompted by his step-mother with all the information needed to find where Captain de la Tour hid his money behind the block-house hill, when he was driven away from Acadia and never came back again. It was darkly whispered that the old Captain did come back on stormy nights, in the time of the spring tides, when the storm winds blew shrilly over the peninsula, and when the night sky was full of wild-driving clouds. At such times, it was said, the old Captain might be seen by anybody who was brave enough to be out in such a night, walking among the spruce-trees behind the block-house hill, muttering to himself, "Where did I put it ? Where did I put it ?"

But, as nobody ever was brave enough to go out to the lonely spruce-covered hill, on such a wild night as I have described, nobody ever did see the ghostly captain. Neither did anybody ever hunt in earnest for the treasure which he was supposed to have buried there.

The expedition of Vene Snowman, Billy and Sam failed, because of an interdict put on it by Mrs. Hetherington. And when Sam's mother caught him hiding three tallow candles under his jacket (these being his contribution to the money-

digging oufit), and made him confess what he was
about, she took him by the ear and led him into the
little bedroom overlooking the bay, and told him
that he should not stir a step out of the house until
it was time for him to go to the pasture after Judge
Nelson's cow.   And, a prisoner there all the bright
afternoon, he was tantalized by the sight of Billy on
the beach below, wondering why Sam, looking out
of the window, frantically motioned him to go
away, but would give no answer to his oft-repeated
whistle-call.   And all this was reason enough why
both boys should remember that there was somebody who did not approve of their having anything whatever to do with incantations and other
such nonsense.

Nevertheless, Billy secretly resolved that he
would find some of Captain Kidd's money when he
grew up, if it was anywhere buried on the Fairport
peninsula.

CHAPTER IV.

THE HOUSE ON THE HILL.

MRS. HETHERINGTON was a tall and stately lady, of whom all the boys of Fairport stood in great awe. She never told Billy to put wood on the fire, but said : " William, you may replenish the fire." Nor was she ever known to refer to Billy's uncle, old Reuben Stover, who lived " off the Neck," as a rich farmer. To her, at least, he was " an opulent agriculturist." And the intimacy which existed between Billy and Sam Black was, according to her, " a distressing social complication with a young person of color." If Mrs. Hetherington had not been famed through all the region around Fairport for her kindness to the poor, her unfailing charity to the sick and the distressed, and for her truly wonderful doughnuts, made by her own white and aristocratic hands, these peculiarities would have been insufferable But no man nor woman who knew—as everybody did—of her great goodness, could think twice of her exceeding fastidiousness.

And no boy who once tasted of those admirable doughnuts, which were given with a liberal hand, could be brought to think that the lady who made them, and gave them away, was anything but a perfect woman. Sam Perkins was wont to say, with a certain appearance of shamefacedness, "Those are better doughnuts than my mother makes, but then, my mother makes the best cupcakes of anybody in the world." This was a great tribute to the genius of Mrs. Hetherington.

The Hetherington house stood on the hill crowned by the old fort. One of the Hetherington ancestors, in the Revolutionary war, had been a general, and he had been brought back here by the British, to his own town, while they held possession of it, and had been imprisoned in the barracks in the fort. The story of his escape and flight across the country to the Penobscot river, accompanied by Captain Wadsworth, an ancestor of one of the greatest of American poets, may be read in the chronicles of Fairport. The home of Billy Hetherington was embellished with many curious relics of those old days. There were the silver-mounted pistols, brought from France, which the Revolutionary hero carried in the holsters of his saddle, and there hung over the mantel-piece the identical sword which General Knox, Washington's trusty lieutenant, gave General Hetherington, with the remark

that no braver man than he ever drew sword in defence of his country's liberties. And in a big ma-
hogany press upstairs, an heirloom in the family,
hung the blue coat faced with buff, and the buff
knee-breeches, which the great man wore for his
uniform when he was at the head of his troops.
The boys of Fairport, admitted to the Judge's
library when that awful personage was absent,
and Billy had the courage to pilot them in, gazed
with awe and admiration on a portrait of Brigadier-
General Hetherington, a tremendous person, indeed,
clad in full uniform, wearing a haughty look and a
long queue, or pigtail, tied with a bow of black
ribbon. It was said that the Hetherington family
burned incense before this work of art, night and
morning, but I do not believe this ; and it is certain
that the old hero stared at the opposite wall with a
fixed and stony gaze, entirely unmindful of the admiration of the boys and of the Hetherington family.

In the days of which I am writing, slavery still
existed in a portion of the United States, and it
had not been long since some of the people who
then lived in Maine could say that they had seen
people who had owned slaves in New England.
And there were dark hints that some of the ancestors of Mrs. Hetherington, whose name was Stover,
had made a great deal of money by bringing slaves
from the coast of Africa to Oldport, Rhode Island,

where they were landed secretly, years and years
ago, when slave-trading and smuggling were regarded with so much abhorrence that nobody liked
to be caught at it.   In the library of the Hetherington mansion was a small collection of queer things
from the coast of Africa, a stuffed parrot, a shield
of wire-grass, a knobby club of iron-wood, and a
frightful-looking spear.   These, ranged against the
north wall of the room, like a trophy of arms, were
supposed by some to have been part of the spoil of
the African captives brought from their native land
by that wicked and remote ancestor of Billy Hetherington, known as " the Black Stover."

None of the Stover family before Mrs. Hetherington had ever lived in the house on the hill.
They had lived in an old and tall house on Main
street, and a straightening of the street, years ago,
had so changed the location of that house that it was
no longer used as a place of residence by anybody.
Once, in the more prosperous times of Fairport, a
portion of the Stover house had been occupied as a
carpenter's shop.   But the carpenter was dead and
gone, the windows of his shop were boarded up,
and timid children, looking in through the chinks
of the boarding, saw, or thought they saw, strange
shapes and monstrous things within, partly revealed
by the few straggling rays of sunlight that found
their way inside.   And at night, only the bravest

of the small boys of Fairport dared to pass on the
side of the street where the old Stover house stood.
There were stories that " Black Stover " had buried
money in the cellar of the old house, and that, on
certain nights in the year, at the time when the
nights were the longest and the days were the
shortest and coldest, the ghost of " Black Stover "
used to come and try to find where his ill-gotten
wealth was buried. This fable delighted and horri-
fied the smaller children very much, and they were
never tired of hearing about the shade of the wild
sea-rover, and of his vain attempts to find his hidden
treasure.

But, though some of the tragic romance of
" Black Stover " was found about the Hetherington
house on the hill, there was a look about the mansion which was so wholesome and hearty that
nobody could long remember the idle stories of the
gossips when the real comfort of the Hetherington
place was in view. The tall Lombardy poplars,
that stood like sentries in front of the house, the
trim flower-garden inside the palings, bright with
hollyhocks, marigolds and china asters, and the
long rows of red and black currant bushes that
stretched in the rear of the mansion, and the lilacs
and seringas that were clumped together before the
front windows, were not at all suggestive of anything
so uncanny as the uneasy ghost of a dead and gone

slave-trader. It was a fine old home, and we may well wonder why Mrs. Hetherington should be afraid that her son Billy should like any other place so much better as to be willing to live elsewhere. But it did really seem as if she thought that Billy would, some day, go off into the wide, wide world with Sam, the colored fielder of the Fairport Nine. It seemed strange that the poor mother should worry so about her boy; but if Blackie had been a rapscallion, instead of the bright and well-behaved youngster he was, Billy's mother could not have been more troubled about her son's intimacy with the only black boy in the village.

"Why, mother," Billy would say, "I don't see why you object to my playing with Blackie. Everybody says that he is the best of all the boys in town, and the schoolmaster, only the other day, said that he was *facile princeps* in the school-room, and in the woods and fields. I don't know what *facile princeps* means, but I know it must be something good, for old Potter thinks Blackie is a bully boy, I am sure. He's always praising him up to the rest of us fellows!"

"My son! my son! what slang! Have I not frequently told you that these low associations would so debase your character and conversation that your family would be ashamed of you?"

Mrs. Hetherington did not object to Billy's play-

ing with poor Sam, but she did object to his being
so much with the black boy. And so when Billy
went out into the back-yard, murmuring to himself, and puzzled as to the reason of his mother's
aversion to Sam, who was the most entertaining
boy in the whole place, to say nothing of the Fairport Nine, he was a little glad to see the object of
his thoughts sitting on the fence which skirted the
Hetherington place next to the fort pasture.

"What's up, Sam?" asked Billy.

"I am," answered Blackie, sententiously. "Leastways, I am up on this fence, and two or three of
the boys are coming up to see us try the walk on
the ceiling."

The boys had been to a circus, lately shown in
North Fairport, and one of the attractions of the
performance had been the feat of " Professor Rinaldo
Rinaldini, the human fly." This wonderful man
had contrived some apparatus by which he had
actually walked on the under side of a plank floor-
ing, head downward, like an enormous two-legged
fly, as Sam Perkins had remarked. While the boys
had been talking over this and other admirable
things which they had seen, Blackie had kept up a
deep thinking, and now that the great base-ball
match was over, he announced that he was ready
to do the feat " as good as the Professor."

Jo Murch and Sam Perkins soon scaled the fence,

and the four boys found "the Lob" in the barn
waiting for the arrival of the performers. The
mow was selected as the scene of operations. I
suppose all country boys know that the mow of a
real barn is the part of the barn which is fenced off,
as it were, from the rest by a deep screen, or fence,
or plank, nearly as high as the eaves of the building. The upper part of this screen is open, but
the lower part is solid boarding or planking. The
mow, or, some call it, the bay, is filled with hay
away up to the eaves, when the hay crop is gathered in the fall. In the summer, however, the mow
is only partly full of hay, and it is great sport to
jump from the beams which cross it, high in the
roof, to the soft and fragrant hay beneath. In the
great barn of the Hetherington place, it was a tremendous leap from the upper beams to the top of
the now half-filled hay-mow. But Sam was equal
to this, and Billy was never far behind him.

On this occasion, however, leaping was not in
order. The game was higher. Professor Rinaldo
Rinaldini was to be imitated. Sam Black had
gathered all the martingale rings that he could find,
and selecting two of the stoutest of these, he fixed
them on the bottom of his bare feet, as he would
have fastened his skates, and he used his skate-
straps for this purpose. Buckling them tight, he
had a ring on the bottom of each foot, strong

enough to hold up a boy of twice his weight; and
Sam was not a very light boy, either. Meantime,
the other boys, under his direction, had nailed
along the under side of one of the beams that
crossed the hay-mow, high up in the roof, several
hooks, once used to drive into the window-frames
of the Stover house, to support the blinds of that
mansion, but now drawn out by the ingenious
Sam. These, driven about a foot apart on the
under side of the beam, were to hold Sam on his
voyage across, in his character as Professor Rinaldo Rinaldini, the human fly.

Sam Perkins, being the captain of the Nine, was
not able to see this performance proceed without
his direction, so, as ring-master, he superintended
the driving of the hooks, and, having examined the
rings and skate-straps on Blackie's feet, to see that
they were all right and tight, he gave the word of
command :

"Now, then, Professor Blinaldo Blinaldinio, you
will please mount the fiery and untamed hay-
mow."

"Get me a couple of halters first," said Blackie.
The halters were brought, and Blackie, neatly spli-
cing them together, climbed up to the topmost beam,
and his halters were thrown up after him. Then,
placing the rope over the beam, he tied the loose
ends underneath, thus making what the sailors call

"the bight of the rope" below the beam. Next,
he slid cautiously down the rope, and, throwing up
his feet, he caught the ring on his right foot into
the first of the row of hooks. Then he slipped the
other ring into the next hook, let go of the rope,
and was off on his walk across the beam, head
downward and feet in the air, precisely like Professor Rinaldo Rinaldini, the human fly. The boys
in the mow below felt their hearts go up into their
throats as they watched Sam painfully move on
from hook to hook.

"What if a hook should pull out?" asked Billy,
with a sinking of the heart. He had not thought
it half so dangerous a feat until now, when he saw
his black crony hanging high in the air from those
rusty blind-hooks.

"Never you fear that," said Sam Perkins, stoutly,
but with a little quaver in his voice: "I drove
those hooks in, and I guess I know a thing or two
about driving things, 'specially when a fellow is going to walk on them."

"Hold on for dear life, professor of the human
fly!" shouted Jo Murch, unpleasantly, for he did
not like to see anybody do anything which he had
not himself done first. But Sam did not need warning. He was now half-way across the dizzy height,
as it seemed to the boys, unused to any very high
places. At that point, a hitch occurred, one of the

hooks being so much bent that it held the ring firmly. The boys all shouted out their advice at once, and Nance Grindle, hearing the racket, came in through the cow-stable, and, unperceived by the excited boys, gazed scornfully at their antics. She was about to give her advice, too, when Blackie disengaged his foot and passed on his perilous journey. Slowly he worked his way across, and in a few minutes more he was on the other side, his left foot in the last hook at the end of the beam, and his face against that side of the barn. Here a new difficulty arose. Sam could not get down! The rope was at the farther end of the beam. His feet could not be taken from the hooks without letting him fall head foremost on the hay, and that would certainly break his neck. Sam Perkins, without knowing why, climbed the joists leading up to the roof, like a cat, and there Blackie hung helplessly in the air, unable to stir. To let go with his feet was almost sure death, and to stay longer, after such a hard feat, was impossible.

Then Nance Grindle, bouncing out of the stall where she had been hidden, cried out :

" You, Sam Perkins ! Get up there and carry Sam Black that rope on the other end of the beam ! Don't you know anything scarcely ? "

Sam was already on the beam, and, without a word, he took the rope, slid it along the beam to

Sam, who grasping it with both hands, held himself firmly for an instant, then, pulling himself upward, loosened his feet from the rings and, turning a somersault, dropped safely, feet first, into the hay-mow below.

"That's the luckiest escape I ever saw," said Captain Sam, from the beam.

"Yes, and you had to have a gal tell you how to get out of it," said Nancy, contemptuously, as she flung out of the barn, half-provoked with herself for having been the means of getting Blackie out of a bad predicament.

"Ever so much obliged to you, Nance!" cried Blackie, as the girl flew off.

"No matter about anything," she replied, without looking back. Then the boys sat down on the hay and talked it all over.

CHAPTER V.

"IF Jake Coombs goes to the mackerel grounds with Captain Kench, I s'pose Pel Snelgro will go too; he always does what Jake does, and then we sha'n't have another hack at the White Bears until next fall, and that's too bad." Sam Perkins said this as he lounged at full length on the hay-mow.

Jo Murch, who was emptying some hay-seed out of his shoe, looked down from his perch on the beam and said: "Say, fellows, I'll tell you what, —let's start a military company." The other boys looked at Jo with amazement, as if unable to grasp his bold idea. Jo was famous for his bold ideas. But Sam Perkins sat up on the hay and cried: "The very thing; let's organize a militia company and call it the Hancock Cadets." Now the name of the local military company was "The Hancock Guards."

"Where shall we get our guns?" asked Billy Hetherington, doubtfully. "A militia company without any guns would be of no account, and we could n't muster more than three altogether, even counting in my father's double-barrelled shot-gun, and I am no way sure that he would let me have that."

" Say, fellows," said Sam Black, " I can fife, you know, and that will be some help, and there is George Bridges, he 's got a drum, or his father has, and that 's all the same, and George drums first-rate ; so there 's the music, anyhow."

Jo Murch, with some little scorn in his face, replied : " Oh, yes, Blackie has got his place in the company all fixed, but he don't show the way to get the arms and 'coutrements."

" What are 'coutrements, anyhow," asked Billy.

" Ignorance ! " sneered Jo. " Why 'coutrements are the things a soldier is obliged to carry. Don't the militia call say, ' armed and equipped as the law directs, with musket, knapsack, priming-wire, brush,' and all that sort of thing ? And the arms and equipments are the accoutrements. Now, then, smarty, ask me another hard question, will you ? "

Here Sam Perkins interposed in the interest of peace.

" I never saw such a disagreeable chap as you are, Jotham Murch ; always trying to be too smart for anything. Why don't you invent something for the arms and 'coutrements ? Say," he added, as a new thought struck him, " we might have wooden swords and guns, you know. I don't believe they would cost much. Charles Fitts is a great dabster in cutting and carving things, and perhaps he would get us up some for next to nothing."

" Pooh!" cried Jo, " who wants to train with wooden guns and broom-handles ? Why, the White Bears would laugh at us, and I should n't blame them, either, if we were to turn out in a rig like that. And say," he said, turning upon Blackie, " you have a great deal of brass to say that George Bridges will be our drummer. Why, he is the White Bears's second base. A nice lot we should be with one of the best basemen of our hereditary foes beating the drum for us," and Jotham leaned over the edge of the hay-mow and jabbed at a stray hen with the pitchfork, in an absent-minded sort of way.

It was explained that George was the only boy in town who had a drum, or a chance at a drum, and that it was necessary that he be invited into the proposed company for his drum ; besides, as Sam Perkins explained, George was a good fellow, and it was not his fault that he was a member of the White Bears's Nine. So it was agreed that he be asked to join the company, when it should be made up, and Sam Black, being a neighbor of the absent _orge, was instructed to give him a chance to come into the organization.

Jo, who had been striking at imaginary hereditary foes with the pitchfork, exclaimed :

"I have it ! Lances are the thing ! When I was in Boston, last summer, I saw the Boston Lancers, and they were just prime. Each man was mounted on a big horse, and he carried in his hand a long lance——"

"But we can't be mounted on horses," interrupted Sam Perkins, derisively. "Besides, where are you going to get your lances, any better than your guns ? "

Sam Perkins did not, as a rule, approve of anything suggested by Jo, and Jo was apt to rebel at the petty tyranny which Captain Sam exercised over the rest of the Nine. And, more than all this, Jo was fond of saying, "When I was in Boston, last year," which was unbearable to boys who had not been in Boston ; and most of the Fairport boys had not been so fortunate. So, when Jo proposed lances, and added insult to injury, so to speak, Sam was ready to quarrel with him. The good-natured rosy-cheeked "Lob" poured oil on the troubled waters, by remarking that lances could be made of long, round sticks, painted and varnished to look like the lances which he had seen in the pictures in Scott's novels.

"But what are you going to do for heads?" demanded Sam Perkins. "Make 'em of cast iron? That would be too costly, and there is no iron foundry in these parts."

"Make 'em of tin," explained Jo, who had recovered his good temper. "Make 'em of tin, and fasten them into the ends of the poles. Tin looks enough like steel to be a lance-head, anyhow, and we can put on some little strips of red bunting to look like the pennons that the Boston Lancers had on theirs."

This, it was agreed, was a feasible plan, and it was settled that the boys should talk the matter over among the members of the Nine, and that they should have a meeting in Hatch's barn, next Saturday afternoon, and at once organize.

The entire Nine, with George Bridges added, met as agreed upon, and it was further and formally agreed that the arms of the company should be lances made as suggested by Jo Murch and "the Lob." The question of the name was not so easily settled. Sam Perkins wanted the name to be "The Fairport Cadets," but Pat Adams said that that was the name of the militia company at Ellsworth. "Why not call it the Fairport Nine?" he cried manfully, mindful of the honor of the base-ball club.

"Why, there will be more than nine of us," said Hi Hatch. "I would n't belong to a company with

only nine fellows in it, and we are ten now, counting George, and he is a member of the other Nine,
besides.   I vote for the name of 'The Hancock
Cadets.'   Ellsworth is a long way off, anyhow, even
if the Captain of the Cadets did say, in his toast,
when the Hancock Guards gave them a dinner on
the common, last year, that it was no further from
Fairport to Ellsworth than from Ellsworth to Fairport.   By the way, fellows, that was a first-rate
toast, was n't it ? ",

"All in favor of calling our company 'The Hancock Cadets,' hold up their hands till counted!"
called out Captain Sam.   Four hands went up,
George's being one.   "Contrary minds!"   Six
hands went up.   "It aint a vote," said Sam, with
some appearance of disappointment.

"Now, then, all you fellows who are in favor of
calling it 'The Fairport Nine,' hold up your hands
till you are counted."   Six hands went up.   "Oh,
this is too ridiculous!" cried Sam.

"Call the contrary minds!" shouted George
Bridges.   "Declare the vote," said Jo Murch, who
had voted for the name of the Nine, just to spite
Sam Perkins, as he afterward explained.   So Sam
declared the name adopted by the company was
"The Fairport Nine"; and "a very ridiculous
name it was, too," as he added, for the benefit of
those who had voted against him.

The election of officers being next in order, Sam 'erkins was naturally chosen captain, though Jo Murch whispered to "the Lob" that there was no sense in making the skipper of a schooner the captain of a full-rigged ship, which figure of speech "the Lob" understood to be a reflection on the policy of choosing the Captain of the Nine as captain of the militia company. "Silence in the ranks!" thundered Captain Sam, as well as his somewhat thin voice could thunder. "Don't begin to put on airs so soon," said Jo. "We're not in ranks yet, and when we are, there will be lots of time for you to put on frills."

Captain Sam wisely overlooked the impertinence, and the election of officers went on, Billy Hetherton being chosen standard-bearer, and Ned Martin first-lieutenant. It was voted not to have any second-lieutenant until the company was bigger. As it was, the rank and file of the company consisted of only five men, or boys, I should say,—the other five being the captain, first-lieutenant, standard-bearer, fifer, and drummer.

"Billy Hetherington ought to have been the captain," said Jo Murch to Blackie, as the boys sauntered homeward, after the election was over. "His father is a judge, and his grandfather was a general," he added, by way of clinching the argument.

"And his mother makes the best doughnuts of anybody in town," added Blackie, with a merry grin. "Is n't that reason enough?"

The first parade of the Fairport Nine took place about two weeks after the organization of the company. It is needless to say that the appearance of the little band was hailed by those of the White Bears who were at home with shouts of derision.

If Captain Sam Perkins's appreciation of military discipline had not been very strong, he would have left the ranks and attacked Eph Mullett with his tin sword, as that unpleasant young man put his head out of the hearse-house door, shouted, "Goose egg!" and shut himself in again.

As it was, Ned Martin, who was not wrapped up in his dignity as he should have been, bawled out: "Nosey! Nosey!" to the mortification of the captain, who shouted: "Silence in the ranks!" until he was red in the face.

Drawn up on the common, the "Nine" mustered fourteen in number, the original ten having been reinforced by four other boys, the smallest of whom was little Sam Murch, whose services in climbing the meeting-house lightning-rod, on the night before the Fourth of July, seemed to deserve some such reward. The lances were resplendent in varnish, and the tin tops, cut out according to a pattern furnished from a picture in *Ivanhoe*, were as

good as the best lance ever put in rest by any of
the heroes of that delightful story,—at least, so
Billy Hetherington thought, as he glanced proudly
at the array. The little strips of red bunting flut-
tered in the breeze from the heads of the lances,
and the general appearance of the troop, as Jo
Murch remarked, was quite like that of the Boston
Lancers. The manual of arms, to which the boys
were somewhat accustomed, after having watched
the militia company of the town at drill, was gone
through very creditably, excepting that " the Lob,"
when told to ground arms, would persist in throwing his weapon on the ground, instead of dropping
the lower end to the ground, as was the customary
fashion in the old-time drill. And Jo Murch, who
was clearly in a mutinous spirit, kept his lance at
the shoulder, when the order " Present arms! " was
shouted by the captain. Captain Sam looked at
the malcontent for a moment, as if in doubt what
to do with him, and then good-naturedly said:
" Well, it is n't any matter, Jo." Whereupon Jo
immediately presented arms, having gained his
point, which was to make the captain " take water,"
as the boys were wont to say.

Another difficulty occurred when the company
was marching to the house of Pat Adams, where
the standard was to be presented to the company.
George Bridges, so intent on beating his drum that

4

he could not keep in line, was continually out of his place, to the confusion of the rest of the troop. Finally, when, absorbed by his own music, he strayed into the grass-grown gutter by the side of the road, Captain Sam came down upon him with his tin sword, and, drawing it from an imaginary scabbard, shrieked:

"If you don't keep in line, I 'll assassinate you!"

To this terrific threat the young drummer, who had about as much idea of the meaning of the word used, as Sam had, replied, with a drawl:

"If you 'sassinate me, I wont drum."

The standard was a magnificent affair, made by the big sisters of several of the boys, assisted by Phœbe Noyes and some of the other girls, who, though they could not lay out the work, were glad to put a few stitches in the beautiful banner. It was made of white cotton cloth, with nine red stars in an oval line, emblematical of the illustrious Nine of Fairport, and in this oval was a cluster of four blue stars, the whole making the old thirteen, the number of the original States. A pair of bright-red curtain-tassels dangled from the top of the staff, which was surmounted by a tin spear-head, gilded, and the whole was a most gorgeous affair.

Flaxen-haired Alice Martin, Ned's sister, had been selected to present the standard. So, with the company drawn up before the front door of the house, pretty Alice, with the flag in her hand, and surrounded by the big girls and the little girls who had had a hand in this business, delivered the following address :

"Soldiers of the illustrious Nine! I am commissioned by the ladies of Fairport to present to you this beautiful banner, whereon are sown the stars of the thirteen colonies of our beloved land. We know we could give it into no more honorable and safe keeping than yours. You are the first to form a company of soldiers among the youth of our beautiful village, and to you belongs the great honor of being the first to receive the flag of your country from those who, though they may not mingle in the fray where you are to win laurels imperishable, may, at least, look on from afar with the sincerest admiration for your prowess, and the most tender wishes for your success in the strife. Take this banner, and, in the words of the poet,—

> "'Forever float that standard sheet,
>   Where breathes the foe but falls before us,
>   With freedom's soil beneath our feet
> . And freedom's banner streaming o'er us.'"

This beautiful and eloquent address, it should be said, was composed by Sam Perkins's big sister Sarah ; and the reply, by the same industrious young lady, was delivered by Billy Hetherington, who, advancing from the ranks, when Alice said " Take this banner," thus delivered his speech :

" Accept my thanks, dear madam,"—and here Alice blushed deeply,—" in behalf of myself and my fellow soldiers, for this elegant testimonial of the interest which the ladies of Fairport take in the welfare of the military service of the Republic. We receive it with pride ; we shall bear it forth with a firm determination to die, if need be,"—and here Billy dropped a furtive tear and his voice quivered a little,--" in defence of the banner thus confidently intrusted to our keeping. When, on the field of battle, or in the lonely bivouac, we shall look upon its shining folds, shining with the stars of our be- loved country, we shall think of this day, when we were reminded by you that, though you may not participate in the strife in which we must engage, you look at the carnage from a distance, and give us your fervent wishes for our success. And, what- ever shall befall, we know that we may depend, in the words of the poet, on this :

> " ' Ah ! never shall the land forget
> How gushed the life-blood of her brave ;
> Gushed, warm with hope and courage yet,
> Upon the soil they sought to save.' "

This address so touched the tender hearts of some of the smallest girls that they choked down a little

THE NINE IN MARTIAL ARRAY.

sob, while Captain Sam, turning to his gallant band, shouted: "Three cheers for the ladies!" The cheers were given with a will, the new banner being waved enthusiastically by the proud and happy standard-bearer.

"Three more for Miss Alice Martin!" shouted the first-lieutenant, her brother. A disorderly and somewhat irregular cheer arose, when Captain Sam, brandishing his sword in air, cried: "Nobody has a right to give orders in this company but me; so, now. Now, then, fellow soldiers! three cheers for Miss Martin, the sister of your brave lieutenant, and the presenter of our flag, which she has done in a beautiful speech." To this long and elaborate command there was an immediate response, and Ned's anger at being reproved melted away.

There was a collation of cakes, pies, and berries and milk laid out in the wood-shed of the house on the hill, and, once more saluting the ladies with three shrill and hearty cheers, the martial Nine filed out into the street, and with fife and drum, colors flying, and lances glittering in the sunlight, they marched up the hill; an admiring throng of girls accompanying them on the sidewalk, they, too, being invited to the feast.

It was a great day for the Fairport Nine, and even Nance, who remained stanch to the prowess of the White Bears, with whom her sympathies naturally belonged, confessed, as she brought out plateful after plateful of Mrs. Hetherington's famous doughnuts, that she was having " an awful good time," the fact that " that black boy was in it all " being the only drawback to her complete enjoyment of the festivities.

CHAPTER VI.

TROUBLE IN THE CAMP.

It was necessary that the first experience of the new military company should be as much like that of real soldiers as possible. It was, accordingly, agreed that there should be what the boys knew as a " muster."

Now, a muster in New England, in these days, was like the annual trainings which are held in some other States. The annual muster in the region of Fairport was held at Orland, a small town a few miles from Fairport. To it resorted all the militia companies from far and near. They were drilled and put through the exercises of war, in the most approved fashion. As the muster lasted for three or four days, it was needful for the soldiers to camp out during their stay ; and so it came to pass that many of the visitors also spent the nights in tents and booths rented for the time by enterprising Yankees of the neighborhood.

The muster was the great annual festival of the

..ng the annual circus in its attractions.
..e travelling jugglers, peep-shows, blow-
..achines, learned pigs, and various delights for
..e entertainment of the visitor ; and the booths,
at which pies, cakes, baked beans, cold roast pig,
ginger-beer, and other delicious things to eat and
drink were sold, were to the boys like a vision of
fairy land. To go to muster was to have a treat
excelled only by a visit to Boston.

Obviously, one lone company could not have a
muster, any more than one bird can flock by himself. But the Fairport Nine did not care very much
for the niceties of military phrase. They would
have a muster, whether it was like the real thing or
not. What does a name signify?

It was late in the summer, and the wild raspber-
ries were ripe, when the boys held their first annual
muster in the block-house pasture of Fairport.
This pasture was on the hillside sloping down to the
shore of Penobscot Bay. The highest point of land
anywhere about that region was once crowned by
a block-house, built by the British at the beginning
of the Revolutionary war. From this eminence
toward the shore, the land descended abruptly, and
the edge overlooking the water was bluffy and pre-
cipitous. But, here and there, among the spruce-
covered hills, were clear spaces level enough for the
Nine (who were really fourteen) to form in line and

in platoons of two and three ; but it was not a good place to march in. The real business of the occasion, however, was the muster.

For several days the boys spent all their spare time in the woods, building the camp. It had been their custom to spend the Fourth of July in camping out, taking a picnic with them. This had been made impossible this year, on account of the playing of the great base-ball match. The muster, too, was to exceed anything of the kind ever before attempted, as the soldiers were to spend the night in camp.

The silent woods resounded with the shouts and calls of the busy boys, who worked harder, as Nance Grindle grimly said, at the building of a camp in the woods than they ever did at any of the home tasks, which they regarded with so much disgust and horror as the very hardest kind of work ever put upon any human being. From the shore was brought many a back-load of drift-wood—long strips of waste lumber and dry poles, to form the frame of the camp. And other back-loads of spruce and fir boughs were brought from the adjacent groves, to thatch the roof and weave into the sides of the structure.

Four or five small-sized trees, standing as nearly as possible in the form of a square, were selected as the corner-posts of the camp, and on these were

4*

nailed the strips of wood and the poles gathered on
the shore, leaving a space for the open door-way.
When the framework was all nailed in place, the
affair looked like a big wooden cage. But when
the fragrant boughs of the fir and spruce were
woven into the frame, concealing the whiteness of
the dry and bleached drift-wood, there was beheld
an arbor of verdure which might well have been the
green nest of some huge bird, so complete and
trim was it.

Inside, the camp (for of course no Fairport boy
could ever have called this an arbor) was lined with
soft twigs of hemlock, and a rude bench of rocks
and shore-worn planks was constructed for the con-
venience of the girls, who were to visit the camp
late in the day. No boy was ever allowed to sit
on these benches, as it was a tradition with the
Fairport boys that this would have been effeminate.

Right merrily worked the boys, the chatter of
their voices and the ringing of their hatchets making
music in the depths of the forest. Occasionally, a
red squirrel paused in his scamper among the trees
to look down with wonder at the busy creatures
who were making such a strange din in the midst
of his haunts ; or a garrulous blue jay perched itself
at a safe distance and scolded violently at the in-
truders. And once, an inquisitive mink, one of the
most timid of animals, stole up from the rocky

shore to discover the cause of all this commotion in the usually silent woods.

"A mink! a mink!" shouted Jo Murch, and away he flew after the beautiful little creature. The mink darted into the mossy crevice of a ledge near at hand, and was gone like a flash. Jo dug his hands into the rough cracks of the rock, as if he would tear them apart and dig out the animal.

"Ho! what a fool Jo Murch is to think that he can catch a mink after it has got into that ledge!" cried Pat Adams.

"You 'd better come here and fix up that brace you burst off when you started after that critter," said Captain Sam, angrily. Now, it must be confessed that Jo was more partial to running after birds and animals than he was to work, even when his labor was that of camp-building, so he replied surlily and threw himself at full length on a heap of spruce-boughs and yawned wearily:

"My! how my back aches!"

"That 's nonsense," said Hi Hatch. "My father says that a boy's back never aches. He thinks it aches, but it does n't."

"Well, I don't care," grumbled Jo. "It feels just as bad to me as if it really did ache; and I am not going to work any more this afternoon, anyhow. That last back-load of lumber that I lugged up from the shore finished me for to-day!"

" If you don't do your share of work, you can't
come to the muster," cried Sam Perkins, who was
boiling with anger at this breach of discipline.

" Ho ! " sneered Jo, " who made you my master, I 'd like to know ? You can't play petty tyrant
on me, now, so don't you try it."

The other boys were aghast at this direct defiance
of the captain. As for Sam, he felt that his authority must be maintained at any cost, so he jumped
down from the roof of the camp, where he had been
arranging the covering of boughs, and clenching his
brown and pitch-covered hands, he advanced toward
Jo, stretched at ease on the bed of boughs, and
before Jo knew what was coming, dealt him a smart
blow under his left ear.

" Now, then, I 'll give you another, if call me
'petty tyrant' again."

Jo, recovering from his surprise, for it was very
seldom that Sam resorted to violence in the maintenance of discipline, was on his feet in an instant.
He gave Sam a blow between the eyes that made
the sparks fly in his brain. But Sam, in an instant,
got Jo Murch by the collar of his short jacket with
his right hand, and his left arm was twisted about
Jo's waist ; his right foot was, meantime, busy with
Jo's legs, trying to trip him to the ground. But Jo
was wary and wiry, and it was several seconds before he fell heavily to the ground, Sam on top.

The other boys looked on admiringly, but with a certain sense of alarm, for this was a real fight, and their gallant commander was not always equal to Jo Murch, who was known as the best "wrastler" in the village.

There was more or less pommelling and scratching in the heap of spruce-boughs around which the rest of the boys gathered at a respectful distance. The two boys fought each other into the open ground and then into a clump of low-growing juniper, in which they struggled with each other in the midst of a cloud of dust which they raised from the dry mass of growth. When the combatants emerged from the confusion and obscurity of the juniper-bush, Sam had Jo's head under his arm, and was pelting the blows into the back of his neck. Presently, Jo, unable to endure this punishment any longer, cried: "I beg!" This was regarded among the Fairport boys as an equivalent for "I surrender," and it was not so difficult to say.

Sam unloosed his hold, and, with a farewell kick, swung loose of his late adversary and looked at him. Somehow, Jo had parted with the greater portion of his jacket, and the only part of his cotton shirt left on him was a stout neck-band of unbleached cloth which was buttoned about his neck. His aspect of sudden raggedness was surprising. But Sam had not come out of the encounter unscathed. He had been working without his jacket, but his shirt was now open behind as well as before, and his satinet waistcoat was a tattered ruin. Blackie picked up the fragments and laid them on a convenient rock, while Sam cooled his flushed face at the spring.

" He 's got a licking that he 'll remember for the rest of this season," spluttered Sam, as he splashed the cold water into his face. " And I 'll give him another whenever he wants one."

" Oh, don't let 's fight any more," said Ned Martin, with a mingled feeling of awe and admiration for his gallant commander.

Jo Murch, gathering up the ragged wreck of his garments, after wiping the blood from his face,—for he had had a blow on his nose,—scrambled up the hillside from the camp, and, shaking his fist at the group below, cried : " You fellows may be bullied around by that petty tyrant of a captain of yours. I wont, and that 's all I 've got to say to him. You can fill my place in the Fairport Nine just as soon as you please ! So, now ! " And with that, and a big rock which he sent crashing through the trees, a moment afterward, Jotham Murch was out of the camping ground, and out of the Fairport Nine.

That night, when Sam had gone to bed in disgrace, and his mother had told the whole shameful story to his father, as she tried to put together the wreck of Sam's satinet waistcoat, 'Squire Perkins only said: " Boys are young animals, Polly. I s'pose they must fight the brutality out of them some time or another."

CHAPTER VII.

THE GRAND MUSTER.

THE camp was finished, and, before dawn one Saturday morning, the Nine, otherwise the martial fourteen, assembled at the old fort as a rendezvous. They came in stragglingly, Captain Sam fretting at the delay. Sam Murch was late, having overslept himself, and there had been rumors that his wicked brother had tied him to the bed-post so that he should not join the Nine in their celebration.

Finally, however, the company started, not in military array, for each soldier was encumbered with a share of camp equipage. No muster could be complete without a genuine camping out, and the valiant Nine had resolved to do everything that should reflect credit on them as real soldiers. They were to start before daylight, as that was the way that the Hancock Guards had to start to go to the muster at Orland. They were to get breakfast in camp, as that, too, was the manner of life on the muster field, and they were to spend one night in

camp, although the smaller boys looked forward to
a night in the woods with secret dread.

It was not a cheerful time of day to begin
operations. The air was chilly, although it was
mid-summer ; and the darkness of the hour, relieved
only by a gray twilight in the east, was somewhat
depressing to the lads, unaccustomed as they were
to being abroad at that time of day. Hi Hatch
confided to his chum, Bill Watson, his belief that
his mother would miss him awfully at breakfast.

At this, Bill, who had a hankering for his usual
comfortable breakfast at home, shivered, and said :
" This is n't half so good fun as I thought it was
agoing to be." Bill was loaded with a frying-pan, a
basket of provisions, and a lance and cartridge-box.
These latter accoutrements were part of his military
outfit, although there was no real reason for carrying the empty cartridge-box in a company of lancers, except for show.

The exercise of walking warmed up the soldiers
to a healthy glow, and when they reached the stone
wall which separated the fort-pasture from " Perkins's Back," as the place of their camping-ground
was called, each boy sturdily declined Captain
Sam's invitation and permission to sit down and
take a rest. They all pressed on to the camp ; but
no boy confided to any other boy his secret fear
that Jo Murch, or some of " The White Bears," had

destroyed their camp in the night. Until the safety of that structure was assured to them, each boy of the party had a sinking feeling right under the middle button of his jacket-front; and it was with a wild hurrah of relief that, having hurried through the last spruce thickets, they came in full view of the camp, which was safe and untouched, in the twilight of the woods.

"It 's all right, fellows!" shouted Sam Perkins, with a gust of joy.

"Of course it 's all right," replied Pat Adams. "Who said it would n't be?"

No boy was willing to confess that he had had any fears on the subject, though each one of them was surprised that the enemy had not destroyed their work, long ago.

"Now, then, my hearties, we 'll have a rousing fire and a hot breakfast, quicker 'n a cat can lick her ear, as my grandpa says!" cried Captain Sam. "Hi Hatch, Sam Black and Billy Hetherington will get up some drift-wood from the shore, Ned Martin and I will build the fire and unpack the grub, and George Bridges and the rest of the fellows will do the cooking. George is boss cook, anyhow."

The boys cheerfully agreed to this last statement, because George, besides being a good-natured fellow, had been to sea, one voyage, and had had some experience in the galley of a coasting schooner.

But there were signs of mutiny at the peremptory orders of Captain Sam.

" 'Pears to me," muttered Billy Hetherington, as the three boys scrambled down the bank to the shore, "that Sam Perkins is putting on a sight of airs. I aint agoing to be ordered about by him all day ; now you just mind."

"Oh, well, Billy," said Blackie, "you know he is captain and we are in camp. What 's to become of military discipline, if we don't obey orders? You know the old saying : ' Obey orders, if you break owners,' and I s'pose that that is just as good for soldiers as for sailors."

"Besides," broke in Sam Murch, "I 'd sooner lug wood than cook. I hate cooking."

The idea that little Sam had ever done enough cooking to have any opinion about it so tickled the other two boys that they burst into a hearty laugh and went to picking up the drift-wood cheerily, and soon clambered back to the dewy hill-side above, where their comrades had already started a fire with the dry litter from the camp-making.

"Sun-up ! Sun-up !" shouted "the Lob," and the yellow rays of the August sun were sifted down among the tree tops, and the distant shore of Long Island was all aflame with the golden light. The

sun cheered the boys, who watched the cooking of
ham and eggs, and coffee, with great interest.
Ned Martin buried potatoes in the ashes, and
burned his hands in getting at them to see if they
were baked.

" Look out, old sorrel-top ! " cried Captain Sam,
good-humoredly ; " you 'll burn your head off, if
you don't take care."

Ned did not like being called sorrel-top, although
his hair was red, but he said nothing more unpleasant in retort than " Drat the fire ! It 's the hottest
fire I ever did see."

" Ned would n't stand that from anybody but
Sam," said Billy Hetherington.

Fortunately, nobody was disposed to discuss this
subject, and breakfast went on right merrily.   It is
true that the coffee was " riley," as the boys said,
not to say muddy, and that some of the ham was
burned to a crisp, and some was nearly raw ; and
there were bits of cinders sprinkled all over the
fried eggs.   But when did a healthy boy's appetite
rebel at such trifles as these ?   Then there were
thick and well-buttered slices of white bread,—the
best bread that any boy's mother ever made,—and
brought to the camp by the different boys who
each had a mother who made the best bread in the
world.

It was even voted that this breakfast was the

noblest meal that any of them had ever eaten in their lives. Hi Hatch sighed no more for the fried hasty-pudding and hot coffee which he knew his sisters at home were, at that moment, eating at his mother's breakfast-table. It was the golden hour of a day in the woods. Such hours do not come to us when we are grown-up men and women.

" I should think we might have just one pie," grumbled "the Lob," who dearly loved pie.

" For shame ! John Kidder Hale ! " said Captain Sam, with all the sternness he could command.

" Aint you a nice fellow to invite a lot of girls to come down here and see our sham-fight, and then go and eat up the pies before they come. Who says pie ? " demanded the captain, looking around on the company, most of whom were lazily basking in the sun. " Who says pie ? " There was no response, although " the Lob " looked about him to see if some other fellow would not help him out with a vote. " Nobody says pie," cried Sam, disdainfully, " and the motion is lost, so now." And that settled it.

Later in the morning, when the camp had been put in order, and the boys had each taken a refreshing dip in the salt sea waves, the lookout in the top of a tall lone pine, Sam Murch, cried : " The girls are in sight, on the top of the hill, back of the fort ! "

Instantly everything was in a tumult of prepara-

tion. It was one of the events of the day when
the girls came to camp.

The company was formed in line, rather a straggling one, to be sure, as the ground was hilly and
broken ; but it was with great pride and satisfaction
that the illustrious and martial Nine, otherwise
fourteen, marched up through the thickets, in single
file, drum beating and fife shrilly playing, to escort
the young ladies to camp. There was the flag at
the head of the column, proudly borne by Billy
Hetherington, standard-bearer, and there marched
Captain Sam, brave in all the glory of a red plume
in his cap and a red sash around his waist. He
brandished his glittering tin sword, crying, as he
did so, "Come on, my brave lads,—the path of duty
is the way to glory !" Nobody knew exactly what
that meant ; even Sam was not sure in his own
mind where he had read it, but it sounded very
fine, for all that.

The girls, approaching from the old fort, saw the
valiant band issue from the woods in bright array,
or in as bright array as the circumstances would
permit. With beaming looks, the fair guests drew
near and stood in a little half-frightened huddle as
Captain Sam shouted, "Attention, company !
Three cheers for the ladies !" The cheers were
given with a will, and the echoing woods repeated
the shrill hurrahs.

"Present arms!" was the next command, and the old soldiers presented their lances in quite exact order, each man holding his weapon perpendicularly in front of his body.

"Now, then, come on, girls," said Sam, wheeling his company about so as to lead the way.

"Well, I should think!" cried Alice Martin. "Why don't you let us go ahead? I don't believe it's good manners for a military company to go before the girls like that. Do you, Phœbe?"

Phœbe Noyes was not sure, but she thought that there ought to be a clear understanding as to what was right before they went on any farther. Sarah Judkins, a tall and freckle-faced girl, whose elder brother was the ensign of the Hancock Guards, and who, for that reason, was an authority in military matters, thought that the soldiers ought to divide and one-half march on each side of the ladies, as they were the guests of the military.

"Just like pall-bearers!" shouted her small brother, Tobias, who was one of the new recruits of the Fairport Nine. "Shut up, sauce-box!" cried Captain Sam. "We'll divide the company, and half shall go before and half behind the girls— ladies, I mean, and that'll be about right." To this Sarah assented, and the procession moved on to the camp.

It was not a very orderly march, as the ground

was rough and it was often necessary for the standard-bearer to lower his flag, in order to pass under the trees. Besides, the girls would talk with the boys in the ranks, and it was in vain that Captain Sam, looking straight ahead into the woods, cried: "Silence in the ranks!" It seemed to the boys almost a week since they had been away from their own homes, and they were anxious to hear what was going on in the village while they had been camping out in the woods.

"That mean Jo Murch says he is coming down to burn down your camp, to-night," said Sarah Judkins, to soothe the feelings of the boy nearest her, who had been saying that the camp was the best ever built in "Perkins's back."

"I'd like to catch him at it!" cried Sam Perkins, forgetting discipline in his rage.

"Silence in the ranks!" screamed Sarah, who had never agreed with Sam since he had given his maple sugar to another girl, right before her face, although it was very well known that he had been going home with Sarah from singing-school nearly all the winter before.

"So I say. Silence in the ranks!" answered Sam, without a blush. Then everybody laughed, and the procession entered the camping-ground, and the military escort was dismissed "for temporary," as the captain graciously explained.

CHAPTER VIII.

HISTORY WITH MODERN IMPROVEMENTS.

THE chief event of the day was to be the sham-fight. The regular militia always had a sham-fight, and the Nine could not possibly think of going through a muster without one. Indeed, the camp had been selected with a view to this very purpose. It was on a tolerably level piece of ground, just above that part of the rocky shore on which the American forces landed, in 1779, when the British held the town and all the rest of the peninsula. From the camp-ground to the shore the land shelved steeply downward; and it was up this high and rugged bluff that the patriot troops clambered and displaced the British.

Billy Hetherington, who had a personal interest in this fight, as one of his ancestors was engaged in it, was of the opinion that it was not much to be proud of. "They got licked like everything, afterward, when they might have taken Fort George, and did n't do it," explained Billy. " And as for

me, I 'd rather be one of the British soldiers, to-day,
because if we ever have another sham-fight on the
old fort, I shall be on hand and drive you fellows
off, just as the British drove Saltonstall, in the
war."

This was felt to be almost treasonable.   No boy
had ever dared to say a word in favor of the British,
whose name was detested in Fairport, although the
Revolutionary War was now a great way behind in
the history of the town.   But, as Billy came of
Revolutionary stock, his patriotism was not to be
made light of, and the other boys wondered at the
amount of his knowledge of those distant events.
It was supposed that he had, somehow, inherited
it from the famous general whose name he bore.
Sarah Judkins, who probably knew more than any
other girl in town, was also able to throw some
light on the matter.

"Land sakes alive!" she cried; "it was not
the fault of the Americans that they did not whip
the British.   It was Satlonstall's fault.   Did n't his
men all want to be led against the British in the
fort, after they had captured this point?   And
did n't Commodore Saltonstall refuse, because he
had been bought with British gold?   Law me!
How you talk!" and Sarah swung her bonnet vigorously by the strings, as was her manner when she
was excited.

" I don't care," broke in Captain Sam, "whether the Americans were defeated afterward or not. They fought like tigers right here, and if they did have to take to their ships and scud off, when they might have captured the fort and taken the town, it was a brave thing to do, anyhow."

" That 's what I say, Sam," said Alice Martin, her blue eyes glistening. " And it was a wicked, wicked thing for those horrid British to chase the Americans in their ships, and drive 'em ashore and wreck 'em all to pieces, as they did, all up and down the Penobscot River."

Here one of the girls reminded the party that Paul Revere, the hero of Longfellow's poem, " The Midnight Ride of Paul Revere," was in command of the ordnance of the ill-fated expedition from Massachusetts Bay, which landed at this place.

" Well, for that matter," said Sarah, who knew everything, " Longfellow's great-grandfather, General Peleg Wadsworth, was second in command, and if he had been first, I just believe he would have got into the fort before the next day, instead of waiting, as Lovell and he had to, until Salton-stall, the coward, gave the word."

She might have added, though every boy in Fairport knew it, that another famous character in that memorable siege was a Lieutenant Moore, of the British 82d Foot, afterward known as Sir John

Moore, who was killed at Corunna, Spain, in 1809. When the school-boys at Fairport recited, as each one of them did as often as permitted, the lines beginning

"Not a drum was heard, not a funeral note."

they felt as if they had had an intimate acquaintance with the brave and unfortunate man who once did subaltern duty in the colonial town, so many years ago.

There was some difficulty in getting members of the company to play the part of British troops, as almost every boy preferred being a patriot soldier on this particular occasion. Sarah volunteered to lead a British column, if none of the boys were willing to serve. This offer so shamed George Bridges that he agreed to be a British soldier for this time only, and Billy Hetherington had already said he preferred that service, having an eye to a victory at some future time.

Blackie naturally joined the company of his chum ; and as there were only fourteen boys, seven on a side, this left but four more to be provided. Sarah Judkins commanded her brother Tobias to fight for the British, which he consented to do, though with a very ill grace. Captain Sam then boldly " conscripted," as he called it, little Sam Murch, Charlie and Tom Tilden to be British defenders.

There was some murmuring in the ranks of the American troops that the newest recruits—Tobias, Charlie, Sam Murch and Tom Tilden—should be selected to fight as British.   It was felt to be an ' intentional slight on these latest additions to the military nine, which was now fourteen.   " Never mind," whispered Tom, who was a gifted fighter ; " we 'll lick 'em, anyhow."

The attacking party, consisting of Captain Sam, his trusty lieutenant, Ned Martin, " the Lob," Hi Hatch, Pat Adams, Bill Watson, and one new re-cruit, Ralph Jackson, were stationed at Trask's rock, for at this point the American patriots were said to have landed.   Tradition says that a fifer boy by the name of Trask, was put behind this big boulder to play his fife while the attacking party made the ascent of the bluff.

Unhappily, Sam Black, the only boy in the Nine who could play the fife, was in the British service at the top of the bluff, and could not be induced to come down and fife for the patriots.   And then the British forces suddenly discovered that they had all the music to themselves.   George Bridges, at a hint from Sarah Judkins, began to beat his drum, before the American forces were ready to begin the attack, and Sam Black blew his fife as well as he could for laughing—it was so funny to think that the besieged party should have all the music.

When Saltonstall's forces, numbering about four
hundred men, landed on this point, in July, 1779,
the marines were on the left of the attack. Captain Sam represented the marines, supported by
"the Lob." Ned Martin, in the centre, kept up an
incessant fire of musketry to distract the attention
of the enemy (see Williamson's *History of Maine*),
while the right, consisting of the rest of the party,
and commanded by Hi Hatch, stormed the British
position, held by Billy Hetherington.

It was a gallant fight!

The British, being posted on the brow of the
steep bluff, had a tremendous advantage. They
poured a galling fire of shouts and cries, occasionally mingled with clumps of wet moss, upon the
heads of the besiegers. The young ladies, who
seemed to sympathize with the British, encouraged
the besieged with remarks upon the slowness with
which the rebels got up the hill.

In the original fight, the right of the attacking
force pressed hard upon the British left and captured a small battery, represented on this occasion
by the standard of the Nine. Hiram, cheered on
by Captain Sam from the left, made a bold dash for
the battery, and was on the point of seizing it, when
Sam Black, indignant at this desecration of the
Nine's standard, snatched it and ran.

"Here! Here! That's no fair play!" shouted

Captain Sam. But Blackie paid no heed to his commander's warning, and Hiram, pursuing the standard-bearer, was stopped by Billy Hetherington, who covered the retreat of his friend with a big wad of wet moss, which struck Hiram full in the face. Hi was too good-natured to resent this, but sat down on the bank and laughed until the tears flowed.

"You're a nice lot of fellows to play American patriots!" exclaimed Captain Sam, angrily. "Why don't you put the invaders to flight? Down with the tyrants!"

But it was in vain. Tom Tilden, at this critical moment, let fly a ball of soft, wet clay, which, taking Captain Sam in the eye, closed that organ for the time being.

Tom shouted in triumph, "Out on the first base!"

At this, Ned Martin, who had kept up his incessant firing, according to orders, by continually bawling "Bang! Bang!" now dropped that branch of the service, and flew up the bluff as well as its shelving surface would permit. He was met at the top by Charlie Mead, who belabored the enemy over the head with a huge bough of spruce. The rough sprays scratched the face of the lieutenant, who made a grab for that weapon and pulled his enemy off the bank, and both rolled together to the bottom, amid the cries of the young lady spectators, who exclaimed :

"Why, they 're fighting ! "

But the two combatants amicably went to Captain Sam's assistance, as he was trying to wash the blue clay out of his eye.

Meantime the contest raged above them, on the bluff. Pat Adams, who saw nothing but a shameful defeat for the American troops, to the great confusion of all history, boldly charged into a group of girls at the top of the bluff, crying, after the manner of Major Pitcairn at Bunker Hill, "Disperse, ye rebels ! Lay down your arms and disperse ! "

But the girls, forgetting that they were not American rebels, nor even British regulars, but peaceful non-combatants, closed around Pat and made him a willing prisoner. Sarah Judkins tied his hands behind him with a handkerchief, and thus exhibited her captive at the edge of the bluff to Captain Sam, who fairly howled at the sight.

Tobias Judkins, having waited for a good opportunity, and assisted by Sam Murch, now loosened a big piece of the projecting bluff, and, in an instant, turf, stones and earth were sliding down the steep bank in a great cloud of dust. The attacking party saw it coming, and fled precipitately down to the shore, dodging the flying rubbish as they ran.

"Oh, I say," cried Captain Sam, "this is no way to fight! We have got to do it according to the original, and in the original, as you ought to know, the British were thrashed."

"Well, if the British were thrashed, why don't you come up and thrash us?" retorted Billy Hetherington, from the top of the bluff.

"Yes ; why don't you come up and drive them out of their battery, just as Lovell's men did?" cried Alice Martin, brightly laughing, for she thought it was a great joke that the American patriots should be asking the British to run away from the threatened battery without making any defence.

"If I could get hold of the fellow that fired that lump of blue clay at me, I'd make him run," retorted Captain Sam, valiantly.

But Ned Martin, not to be defeated in this way, had made a circuit to the extreme right, though not according to the original plan for which the captain was such a stickler. Before anybody knew where he was, and in the midst of the parley, he appeared behind the party on the bluff, waving the standard, which he had found in the bushes, and exclaiming, "I 've captured the battery!"

There was a rush of boys in this direction, and the whole party fought their way to the edge of the bluff. "The Lob," supported by Ralph Jackson,

5*

who was a big boy, climbed up to aid their struggling lieutenant.

They were all tangled together on the dangerous
edge of the bank, when the captain from below
yelled, "Look out! The bank is caving!"

His warning was too late. In another second,
the edge of the bank gave way, and amid dust and
dirt, the shrieks of the girls and the cries of the
boy-besiegers below, the entire force of British and
Americans slid down to the rocky shore beneath.
There were bruised heads and shins, and Pat
Adam's nose was bleeding when he picked himself
up. Most serious disaster of all, however, the pole
of the standard was broken into two pieces, at sight
of which the girls came hurrying down, with various
exclamations.

"It is too awful mean for anything," pouted
Phœbe Noyes, who, having done much sewing on
the banner, felt as if she were personally wounded
in its disaster.

"It's all your fault, Billy!" cried Ned, fiercely.

"'Tis n't my fault, either," retorted Billy. "Do
you s'pose I was agoing to let you carry off that
flag?"

"Why, that's the way the fight was fit in 1779,"
answered Captain Sam. "What are you thinking
about!"

"Well," remarked Sarah Judkins, gravely, "the

fight is over and the Americans have got the worst of it."

"That 's so," gallantly assented Sam. "It 's not according to the original, but the enemy being assisted by the ladies, the patriot forces are beaten."

CHAPTER IX.

A MIDNIGHT ATTACK.

THAT night, when the feast was over, and the girls had gone home, and the darkness of the wood was only dimly lighted by the flickering flames of the bonfire, the old soldiers were not only tired and sleepy, but somewhat lonely. To be sure, there were fourteen sturdy boys of them, and as they began to select their sleeping-places for the night, they had a feeling of being very much more numerous than they were. Every boy wanted to sleep in the best place, and, as there were not many best places, it was difficult for so many to be accommodated. But this nice question having been adjusted by Captain Sam, who solved all difficulties by taking the best berth for himself, the boys lingered around the fire, loath to go, and yet reluctant to sit up longer.

"I'll tell you what it is, fellows," said Blackie, "this would be a first-rate chance to go money-digging. None of our folks would know a word about it, and we might go over to the fort-pasture, where that ring is made in the turf, and try our luck."

"Pshaw!" cried Captain Sam, scornfully, "What's the use of going after old De la Tour's money on a night like this? See, there isn't a cloud in the sky. You can't dig for money on a clear night. It's got to be cloudy, but with the moon at the full, and the wind must blow a ten-knot breeze at the very least."

"Besides," added Billy Hetherington, "we have n't got any tools."

"But there is a spade and shovel, and then we have two hatchets in the camp. And that's all we want."

"But," explained Billy, "we want money-digging tools. We must have a divining-rod, and the seven white feathers from a field-sparrow's tail, and lots of things besides." There was a general laugh at this, as most of the boys, although they had heard of the magical tricks and tools supposed by the ignorant and superstitious to be necessary for money-digging, were ready to ridicule all such notions when they were seriously discussed. Billy reddened at the laughter which he had raised by his earnest remark, but, as he screened his cheeks from the hot glare of the fire, he said, a little petu-lantly, "Well, you may laugh, but I have heard

old Ma'am Heath tell how old Kench found that
treasure over on the Doshen shore, with a divining-
rod and other things."

" And she told how a big, black dog, with red,
fiery eyes, came and barked at old Kench, as he
was digging, and how the old man said : ' What 's
that ? ' And then the lights all went out, and how
the chest, which he could just feel with the end of
his shovel, went down, down." This was Hi
Hatch's contribution to the learning of the money-
diggers. And, as he told his tale,—told so many
times before,—the boys looked suspiciously around
them into the gloomy depths of the wood.

" Oh, pshaw ! " cried Ned Martin, " what 's the
use of talking such rubbish ? You 'll scare these
little fellows so that they wont dare to go to bed
to-night. There is little Sam Murch, now, so scared
that his eyes are sticking out so that you can hang
your cap on them."

Sam stoutly denied that he was frightened the
least bit, but his teeth chattered as he spoke, and
some of the other small boys declared that it was
growing cold. So, with many protests that they
were not sleepy, the party curled up in twos and
threes on the layers of fragrant spruce and cedar
boughs with which they had covered the uneven
floor of their camp.

Billy Hetherington and Blackie nestled close to

each other, and whispered for a while about the money-digging project which was so dear to Billy's heart. But Blackie soon dropped off to sleep, and all the camp was still, to Billy's wakeful ear, save when some little chap, turning uneasily, muttered in his dreams.

The fire snapped and flickered outside the camp. The white rays of the moon began to sift down through the tree-tops, and afar off on the bay could be heard the rude music of sailors singing as they hove up anchor, a sound which was comforting to Billy, who lay still and thought of the ship which had anchored there in the afternoon, waiting for the turn of the tide to take her up to the port. Then the cheery "Yo-heave-ho" of the sailors died away, and the listening boy heard only the snapping of the hemlock in the fire, and the distant and mournful cry of a loon on the bay. Occasionally, too, a night-hawk gave a shrill call as he whirred over the forest, or the hoot of an owl sounded and resounded dismally from the Block-house hill.

"Why can't I get to sleep?" moaned Billy, impatiently to himself. "There's Sam actually snoring. Oh, dear! oh, dear! Why can't I get to sleep? I wonder what the folks are doing at 'home? It's after nine o'clock. We heard the meeting-house bell ring ever so long ago. I s'pose

Old Fitts is sound asleep by this time. Oh, dear me! Why can't I get to sleep?"

The boy raised himself up and looked enviously around on his sleeping comrades. Little Sam Murch was lying where a ray of white moonlight fell across his face, and Billy mused:

"He 's a nice boy, Sam. I wonder why he is such a good chap, and his brother is such a slouch? I wonder if Jo will join the White Bears? I wonder if we wont lick the White Bears, the next time we have a match game with them? That was an awful good catch that dear old Blackie made, last game. Oh, dear! oh, dear! Why don't I go to sleep? There! The moon is shining right spang in Sam's face. I wonder if it will strike him blind? That 's what old Tumble says. I wonder if old Tumble would know how to dig for money? I wonder if the White Bears would come down and break up our camp to-night, if they knew we did not stand guard, as they do up to Orland when they have muster there?"

And here Billy, in sheer desperation, lay down and went to sleep. At least, he thought he had gone to sleep, when he heard a soft tread outside. Instantly, he was alert and listening. Again he heard it. Was it old De la Tour coming back for his money? But the old captain did not haunt this part of the peninsula; besides, he did not usually come at this time of year. There were whispers in the darkness, and Billy felt cold chills running down his back, and a goose-fleshy feeling all over him. There was a tight band around his head, and he felt that his hair was standing on end. Scared though he was, he had enough presence of mind to wonder to himself if his hair was really standing up, or if it only felt so. Then he poked Blackie in the back, and, as the lad turned sleepily, he whispered in his ear:

" There 's somebody outside of the camp ! "

" White Bears," suggested Blackie.

" I guess so," replied Billy. " Listen ! "

And Blackie listened. Just then, a big stone came crashing through the side of the camp, and struck Tom Tilden in the back. That warrior awoke with a tremendous howl of rage and pain. With that, the cry of " Firebrand ! Firebrand ! " rang through the woods, and the Fairport Nine knew that the Philistines were upon them. The battle-cry of the White Bears was " Firebrand ! " Why, nobody knew, but when the sleeping camp was aroused by that ominous yell, they knew who were their assailants. Even in the dark, it is a good thing to know with whom you are fighting.

" The enemy are upon us ! " shouted Captain Sam, not forgetting his position as commander, even in the midst of alarms. " The enemy are upon us ! Charge bayonets ! "

There were no bayonets to charge with, and, even if the Nine had had them, the enemy were not to be seen. When the boys rushed out into the open, where the fire was dying down into embers, nobody was to be seen. There was not a sound of the enemy.

"Come out of your hiding-place, you cowards!" shouted Captain Sam, valiantly. They waited for a moment to see if anybody would break cover. Then a voice in the darkness replied:

"Oh, hush up, you petty tyrant!"

Then everybody knew that Jo Murch had gone over to the White Bears.

This insult to the captain was more than he could bear. He rushed into the shadow of the wood from which the voice had come, and, belaboring the thicket with a thick stick, he presently uttered a loud yell and rushed back to camp with a bleeding nose.

"First blood for the White Bears!" shouted a voice, derisively, from behind a clump of spruce-trees.

Billy Hetherington, flying in the direction of the sound, saw Joe Fitts, the centre-fielder of the White Bears, sneaking around to get into the camp. Without thinking of the bigness of Joe, who was twice as tall as Billy, the boy threw himself on him, crying: "A spy in the camp! A spy in the camp!" In another moment the two boys were wrestling on the ground, Billy underneath. But Blackie was not far off, and, before Joe Fitts could turn his head to see what had happened, the agile black boy was on his back, pommelling him with a very fair-sized fist. Joe roared for mercy, and, in the midst of the tumult, Tom Tilden came up, and Joe was made a prisoner.

"First prisoner for the Fairports!" now shouted Captain Sam, in derision, to the hidden White Bears. His only answer was a big stone that came whirling out of the bushes and fell, without any injury to anybody, into the fire, which was now heaped up with fuel.

Joe Fitts, the prisoner, contentedly sitting by the cheerful blaze, refused to give any account of the numbers and purposes of the White Bears. "You know, fellows," he explained, "it would n't be the fair thing for me to tell on my own crowd, and you had n't ought to ask me, now, and you know it."

Billy suggested that their prisoner might be put to torture, as once was the custom in warfare.

"Tie him to a tree and stick splinters into him," suggested Hi Hatch, who was a deeply learned reader of Indian massacres and Indian fights. Tom Tilden, who had great admiration of his own fighting prowess, invited the captive to a rough-

and-tumble wrestle, no tripping, underhold, and no
biting nor pulling hair. This contest was sternly
forbidden by the captain, and Joe was tied to a
birch-sapling to wait for developments.

It was now past midnight, and the moon had
begun to sink in the west. The air was chill, and
the excited boys were cooling off, as the attack had,
somehow, ceased. The besieged party were un-
certain what to do. " Let's make a charge into
the woods and rout them out," said " the Lob,"
who was too clumsy to fight, although he was the
champion catcher of the Nine.

Just then, a strange thing happened.

The camp was built with one side toward the
shore, which was below, at the base of the rocky
and wooded bluff. In front of the camp was a
cleared space, in which burned the camp-fire, and
all around, and beyond, where the broken ground
finally rose to a considerable height, were thickets
of spruce, hemlock, fir and pine, with a few tall
and thick beeches and birches mingled in between.
Suddenly, from the darkest portion of the wood opposite the door of the camp, emerged a solitary figure.   It was that of an old man dressed all in black,
with a cocked, or three-cornered, hat on his head,
and with white hair hanging down on his shoulders.
His face was covered by a full black beard, and
everything about him was black, except his hair and

a red feather in his hat. Bright buckles glistened at the knees of his small-clothes, and in his hand he carried a gigantic cutlass. This strange figure, emerging from the darkness of the wood, stopped short when it had reached the open space, farthest from the fire. Then it waved the cutlass three times in the air, and remained motionless.

Breaking the painful silence, Joe Fitts, tied to the sapling, ejaculated : " The Black Stover, as I'm alive !"

At this the figure waved its cutlass three times again, as if to say this was correct. The boys gazed spell-bound for a moment, when Captain Sam, with a perceptible quaver in his voice, shouted " Who are you ? " The figure made no other reply than to point downward to the ground with its cutlass, as if digging, and then, turning, it was about to vanish into the woods, when Ned Martin and Tom Tilden rushed forward swiftly and silently and, without a word of warning, grabbed the spectre by the legs and brought him to the ground with a tremendous thud. That ghost must have weighed at least one hundred and ten pounds. Instantly, as it fell, a crowd of White Bears plunged from the wood and threw themselves on Tilden and Martin, who manfully resisted every effort of the ghost to get away, helped though it was by its comrades. A re-enforcement from the camp now rushed up,

and Captain Sam, throwing himself into the struggling heap of boys, tore from the head of the appa-
rition a wig of hemp and a massive set of whiskers
made of black moss.   He was proceeding to insult
the ghost of the Black Stover still further, when
that discomforted spectre cried, in the unmistakable
language of a White Bear and a Mullett : " I surrender, fellers ! Le' me up ! "   So the ghost got
up, with his nose bleeding profusely, and disclosing
the   familiar   form   of   Eph   Mullett,   otherwise
" Nosey."   It was Ephraim's habit to talk through
his nose.

" Second blood for the Fairport Nine," observed
Pat Adams, gravely.   The White Bears acknowledged themselves defeated, " for once," they said,
with an unpleasant attempt at sarcasm.   So a truce
was sounded, and the late combatants sat down
around the fire, and discussed the battle with great
friendliness.

"Oh, were n't you fellers just scared out of your
wits, though ? " said Peletiah Snelgro.

" No, we were not," answered little Sam Murch,
who had stood guard over the prisoner while the
rest of the force went to the attack on the ghost.
At this, everybody laughed good-humoredly, except
Jo Murch, who kept at a distance from Captain
Sam, and who did not think that his small brother
had any business in the camp of the Nine, anyhow.

"Well," said Billy, "I 'll own up that . scared when I heard the whisperings and the treau. about in the darkness and the night, when all the rest of the fellows were sound asleep and snoring."

"Snoring! Come now, I like that!" cried Hi Hatch. "I never snore. No fellow ever snores. Leastways, I never knew anybody who owned up that they did."

"It was n't the snoring that frightened you," said Dan Morey, the left fielder of the White Bears. "It was the ghost of the Black Stover a-coming after his buried treasure."

"Just as though anybody could n't tell that that was a real fellow!" sneered Ned Martin, who was not a little proud of the courage and presence of mind with which he had assaulted the ghost.

"Well," yawned the spectre, "I don't know how it is with you chaps, but I am clean beat out, and have n't been so sleepy since the wreck of the "Royal Tar." The "Royal Tar" was a steamship which had been burned on the bay, at a date when some of the smaller boys were too young to know much about it, although they had been told, in later years, of the horrible sight of the wild beasts of a menagerie which was on board, leaping from the burning cages and plunging into the waters of the bay to perish. So, when Eph said that he had not been so sleepy since the wreck of the "Royal

Tar," and it was known that he had sat up all night to see the wonderful and tragical fire, they felt for him an immense respect.

"Well, I was only four years old when the 'Royal Tar' was burned," said Hi Hatch, "but I can lick any fellow who says I am not sleepy." So saying, he looked around and met no answer but a general chorus of yawns.

Even the sound of the night-birds was hushed, and the white streaks of the dawn were paling the eastern sky, as besiegers and besieged, friends and foes, White Bears and Fairports, lay down together and slept peacefully around the smoldering fire.

CHAPTER X.

THE MONEY-DIGGERS.

A FEW days after the great muster and camping-out of the Nine, Billy and Blackie lounged into the village apothecary's shop. It was a curious old place, highly attractive to the boys on account of its being the only shop in town where stick licorice, snake-root, gamboge, and other things necessary to a boy's happiness, were sold. On the shelves, too, were ranged glass jars, known as " specie jars," filled with sticks of peppermint and sassafras candy, and in the back shop, aromatic and pungent with strange odors, were produced divers sweet and palatable syrups recommended for coughs and colds, and so greatly relished by the children of the village that they sometimes aggravated their slight disorders for the sake of having a dose of one of these honeyed mixtures.

"Now, that's a mighty cur'ous coin," said the apothecary, a tall, spare and bald man, wearing a pair of tremendous spectacles on his nose. It was

6

a silver coin, about as large as a quarter of a dollar,
but much thinner.   On one side was a rude represen-
tation of a pine-tree, with an illegible inscription
about the rim.   On its other side was the inscription " New England—An—Dom," and in the centre of this the date, " 1652," under which were the
numerals, " XII."

"Yes; a mighty cur'ous coin," repeated Mr.
Redman, slowly.   " How did you ever come across
that, Abel ? "

Now Abel Grindle was a close-fisted and close-
mouthed old farmer who lived " off the Neck," as
that portion of the main-land immediately adjoin-
ing the peninsula of Fairport was called.   And to
Redman's question he replied : " I don't know
that it makes the leastest mite of difference to you
where I got it from.   Duz it ?   It 's good money.
Wuth a shilling, ain't it ?   Looks to me as if 't was,
and I cal'late I know good money when I see it.
It 's wuth a half a pound of rat-p'ison, anyways, and
that 's all I want to-day.   Rat-p'ison haint riz, has
it, Mr. Redman ? "

"Why, it 's a Pine-Tree shilling ! " exclaimed
Billy, who had managed to get a sight of the coin
which the druggist was turning to the light.   " My
father has got one of them, which his grandfather
had.   That was coined by the Province of Massachusetts, ever so long ago, when Maine was a part

of Massachusetts, and Massachusetts had n't set up for herself."

Billy paused, with his face flushed at his boldness, as well as with excitement over the discovery of a Pine-Tree shilling being offered "in trade" for rat-poison.

"Smart boy," said the apothecary, looking approvingly at Billy over his spectacles.

"Too pesky smart for anything," muttered the farmer.

"If you know so much, youngster, perhaps you can tell me what this is," and the old man displayed on the palm of his dingy, seamed and horny hand an irregularly shaped lump of silver which looked as though it had been hammered out flat and then stamped. It was thick in the middle, and thinner at the edges. On one face was stamped something which looked like a Greek cross, in two angles of which were two queer-looking creatures, rearing on their hind legs, and probably meant for rampant lions. In the other two angles of the cross were castles, and scattered over the piece were letters, but so worn that they could hardly be read. The other face of the strange coin bore a complicated design, and the only parts of it which could be made out were two upright pillars, bearing something like leaves on their tops.

"That 's the Spanish pillars, fast enough," said

the apothecary, musingly. "And that 'Hisp' must mean Spanish, I cal'late. Put your sharp eyes onto it, Billy."

"I 'm afraid I don't know what this is," said Billy, modestly, "but those are the Spanish pillars, sure enough, and oh! here 's the date! 1667! Why, what an old fellow it is!"

Now Blackie, taking the coin into his hand, cried:

"Aha! I know what this is! It 's what we read about in *The Pirate's Own Book*. Don't you remember, Billy, those 'pieces of eight'? I don't know why they were called 'pieces of eight,' though; there is a big 8, and a 'P,' and an 'E' right up there between those pillars. Some folks call them cob dollars, I don't know why, unless Gen. Cobb first dug 'em up, for they are mostly dug up."

"The nigger is a smarter boy than the other one," said Abel Grindle, with a sour smile. "They were dug up, every one on 'em, on my farm off the Neck."

The eyes of both boys fairly shone with amazement at this tale. But the apothecary only put his spectacles on top of his bald head and said: "Land sakes alive! You don't say so." In New England, at least in those days, it was not the custom of the people to be surprised by anything.

Before night, the entire population of Fairport

knew that Abel Grindle had found on his farm several thousand pieces of silver money. Some said that there were two thousand dollars, and some said that he had found ten thousand dollars in gold and silver. The truth was that he had found about two thousand pieces, but many of them were very small, scarcely as large as the fourpence ha'penny, or six-and-a-quarter-cents coin, which circulated then. But in the treasure were many of the big thick "pieces of eight" which Sam Black had described; and then there were Pine-Tree shillings and sixpences, French crowns, half-crowns, and quarter-crowns, besides numerous coins of Spanish and Portuguese origin, the original value of which nobody knew.

Abel Grindle had been picking up the rocks and stones which plentifully covered his fields, when, turning over a flat rock, " about as big as a bake-kettle cover," as he expressed it, his astonished eyes fell on a heap of coins, tarnished and dusty, but showing that they were once good, honest money. Nobody could tell who had put them there, but public opinion, after the excitement had somewhat subsided, settled down to the belief that this was some of the " Black Stover's " ill-gotten gains. And more than one ancient gossip, shaking her head wisely, said that " it was master strange that Mrs. Hetherington's son should be the first to have a good square look at the money which her grandfather had hid away in the ground."

As for Billy, his imagination was fired anew by this wonderful discovery. In their secret talks, he and his black chum discussed the matter so earnestly that they finally resolved to try their luck at money-digging. Many an expedition through the pastures did the youngsters have before they could make up their minds where to dig. There was scarcely a spot on the entire peninsula which did not have a history to it. All around the old Fort George were marks and scars of the battles of the Revolution ; and in the fort-field, as it was called, the plow of the farmer often turned up a brass button with a big " 82 " on its rusty surface, showing that it belonged to the uniform of some poor soldier of His Britannic Majesty's 82d foot.

Down by the shore, below the town, were the ruins of the old French fort, built by the exiled baron, who, in 1667, established himself here, and married an Indian wife from the tribe of the Tarratines. Near by, too, was the very spot on which the pirate, Gibbs, was said to have landed to hide in the earth the rich booty which he had taken from the traders of the Spanish Main and the West Indies. Near the light-house, farther down the shore, and toward the entrance of the bay, were mysterious caves and fissures in the rocky precipices of the bluffs, in which dark deeds were said to have been done in ancient times. And on the top of Block-house Hill were the remnants of an old foundation, under which it was said and believed that the British had hidden the plunder of rich prizes captured along the coast, and which they had left behind them in the hurry of their flight, when they finally left this part of the country.

All over the pastures were low rings of earth, usually about fifteen feet in diameter, where once had been what seemed miniature forts. But these were too small for any warlike purpose. Besides, they were scattered about without any reference to the forts and batteries which had been built in the old times by the fighting races that, one after another, had occupied the peninsula. Nobody could guess why these mysterious rings on the surface of the earth had been made. Billy and Sam, after much debate and hard thinking, came to the conclusion that they marked spots where money was buried.

At some time in his life, every Fairport boy had tried his hand at money-digging. Blackie and Billy, when they resolved to try theirs, came to the sensible conclusion that it was not worth while to bother with incantations and spells. Here was old Abel Grindle, who, while Ma'am Heath and the rest of the wise ghost-seers were trying magic spells and hunting for buried treasure with divining-rods, had actually turned up a heap of money, in broad daylight, and while he was engaged in the particularly hard and commonplace work of picking up rocks on his farm.

Nevertheless, it was thought safest, almost necessary, to dig for money at night, and as near midnight as possible; so, with much secrecy, the two boys smuggled into the orchard behind the Hetherington house a pickaxe, two shovels, and a crowbar. To these were added several tallow candles, a ball of twine, and a meal-bag, in which the treasure was to be carried home.

Now it chanced that on the very night which Billy and Sam had chosen for their secret expedition, Captain Sam Perkins and his trusty lieutenant, Ned Martin, had resolved to carry out a long-cherished piece of mischief. In front of the old fort above the town lay an ancient gun, a twenty-four-pounder, which had been left to rust and decay ever since the fort was dismantled. Children played about its black muzzle, and the birds of the field billed and flirted with each other at the vent where once flashed the ill-omened fire. On one Fourth of July, some of the patriotic citizens lifted the mouth of the cannon from the grass and put a big stone under its muzzle, and fired it in honor of the day. So there it lay, and the two boys, furtively hoarding their powder, and hiding it in the hay-loft for weeks and weeks, finally got together enough to load the old piece once.

It was a dark night when Sam and Ned, who had slept together at Ned's house, as being nearest the fort, slipped out of bed, down the water-conductor, and off to the fort. As they crept by Deacon Adams's house, they heard the tall old clock in his front entry strike twelve. They shivered. The night was not very cold. Quickly was the cannon loaded with grass, wet moss, and anything that would "make the old thing speak." A slow match was slipped into the touch-hole, and back to the house, up the conductor, and into bed, went the young artillerymen. Then they lay and waited in breathless silence for the report which did not come.

Meanwhile, the two money-diggers, meeting at the appointed apple tree in the Hetherington orchard, gathered up their tools, and swiftly and silently sped across the fields to the old fort. At the south of the fort was the earth-ring which the boys had selected for their operations. It was fourteen feet across, and not more than nine inches above the level of the ground. Stretching two lengths of string across from four points opposite each other on the outer rim of the circle, they found the middle of the ring at the place where

6*

these crossed each other. It had been decided
that it was necessary to dig for money in the middle.

"Now you go it with the pick, and I will handle
the shovel," whispered Sam. "And when I make
motions with my hands, so, you take the shovel for
a spell." For it had also been decided that it was
absolutely necessary that not a word should be said
while the digging was going on.

It was hard work, and the boys, who had been
shivering in the cold, moist air, were soon in a glow
of perspiration. They stopped to breathe, peering
down into the hole, already nearly two feet deep,
when off in the darkness somewhere they heard a
muffled thud, as of somebody ramming down a
cannon. Sam shivered and shook perceptibly.
Billy put his finger warningly on his lips. Then
they exchanged glances, for they knew that that was
only a trick of the ghostly guardian of the buried
treasure to make them speak. But, as they bent
to their work again, each boy felt a chilly sensation
glide down his backbone.

A few minutes later, Sam and Ned, turning uneasily in Ned's bed, wondered why that cannon did
not go off. It seemed to them that it had been an
hour since they left the fort. Really, it was not
fifteen minutes.

"We might as well go up and see what 's the

matter, Ned. It 'll never do to let the load stay in until to-morrow."

Sam's right leg was already out of the window when a prodigious explosion took place. It seemed as if the town were blown up by a mine underneath. Then there was a sound of jingling glass from windows broken by the concussion. Then other windows were heard opening in the darkness. Anxious female voices called across the street to village neighbors, asking " what the land-a-massy's sake had happened." Then there were the patterings of many feet on the wooden sidewalks. But nobody knew where to look for the cause of the frightful explosion. Probably, thought some of the timid folks, it was an earthquake.

Blackie and Billy were hard at work, Blackie digging and Billy shovelling. They had a good-sized hole made in the earth, and no goblin had come to disturb them. Awkwardly handling his shovel, Billy smote his chum a hard blow on his toe. Sam, smarting with pain, dropped his pick, and, grasping his wounded toe in his hand, cried : "Ouch!" In an instant, the air was red with flame, and a tremendous peal of thunder, louder than any cannon, burst in the direction of the front of the old fort. There was a rattle of something jingling, and then all was still. The only sound in that part of the fort-pasture was the swift brushing of bare feet through the dewy grass, as two badly scared boys darted across the hill, flew over the stone wall, scudded through the orchard, and finally buried themselves deep down in the hay in Judge Hetherington's barn. So deep did they bury themselves that they did not hear the voice of the Judge calling, "William, my son, where are you?"

So deep did they bury themselves that when, next morning, Reuben Gray, the hired man, trampling over the hay, felt something lumpy underfoot, dragged out first a black boy, then a white one, both of these, sitting up, said, as in a chorus, "Was it an earthquake?"

CHAPTER XI.

NED MARTIN, Billy Hetherington, and Blackie had formed, during a previous summer, a private company, so to speak, for the maintenance of an imaginary kingdom. They were boys of vivid imagination and fancy, and it was easy for them to contrive all sorts of adventures in which they took part. But the central idea of the whole thing was an imaginary State, which they called the kingdom of Pedan. Where they found the name of their kingdom, none of them could tell. Like many other boys, they "made it up as they went along." Out of books of history and adventure, which they read with great eagerness, the three boys drew the materials for the campaigns, battles, and other surprising events, which they went through with whenever they "played Pedan," for this game was a favorite one with them when they were left to themselves.

There was, of course, an imaginary king of this

imaginary kingdom, but he was never spoken of
otherwise than as " the king." He never made his
appearance except in imagination, and when the
boys made believe very hard, they could see, or
think that they saw, the King of Pedan, in all his
state and glory, rewarding them for great deeds
done in the defence of his kingdom and crown,
for the king was forever at war with somebody.
Ned Martin was the general-in-chief of the Pedan
army, and Billy and Blackie were the two next in
command. It was in vain that Ned declared that
there could not be two of an equal rank in the
army. There must be one major-general who
should outrank the other, but to this distinction
neither Billy nor Blackie would agree. Neither
would consent to outrank the other. And so the
three generals went to war, whenever they had a
chance, with equal rank, and each one commanded
his imaginary forces in the field without the least
clashing or jealousy of the others. It was the custom of the three boys to make believe that the
kingdom of Pedan was chiefly situated around Mr.
Martin's orchard and the adjacent fields. In the
rear of the big red barn was the principal city of
the kingdom, which was known as Borax. Along
a drain (which was known as the River Pedan)
was situated the city of Bias, and beneath the
crooked apple-tree at the foot of the orchard was

the city of Butler. Hard by the well was the city of Border. All of these titles were taken from the spelling-book, in the column of words of two syllables, beginning with B.

The King of Pedan was forever at war, and his generals had a hard time of it. In fact, their principal business was fighting imaginary foes. When the boys came out of school, of a summer afternoon, inflamed with the exploits of the Trojan hosts, and with the doings of Hector, Achilles, and the other heroes whom they found in their Latin lessons, it was the most natural thing in the world for them to repeat the siege of Troy, or the battles of the contending races immortalized in the Iliad and the Odyssey.

But the most troublesome foe of the King of Pedan was the King of the Numbfudgeons. The Numbfudgeons were a warlike race who inhabited a thicket just beyond a line of currant-bushes, at the bottom of the orchard. This thicket was filled with imaginary enemies, all Numbfudgeons, of course, and it was only when they broke over into the orchard and advanced beyond the line of the currant bushes, that they were in plain sight, or imaginary view, of the valiant defenders of the kingdom of Pedan. Then the outcry was tremendous. Each of the three boys, shouting at the top of his voice, charged into the ranks of the foe, laying about him with his weapon in every possible direction, and cheering on his men with cries referring to their altars and their fires, as near as possible in the manner laid down in the story-books and histories.

The principal weapon of the Pedanites, however, was one known as the grumgrudgeon. This was, in fact, a stout club or cudgel. But, in imagination, it was a terrible affair. To the excited fancy of the boy who wielded it, it was a sword, a pike, a gun with terrible powers, and a telescope through which the enemy could be seen approaching from a distance. Armed with this wonderful engine, the three great generals of the kingdom of Pedan were wont to slay their thousands and tens of thousands, and to take any number of prisoners, every time they went into battle. And they were in battle array nearly all the time when they were playing Pedan, as I have already said.

A great flat rock, in the west corner of the orchard, was the scene of many naval engagements between the fleets of Pedan and Numbfudgeon. For both nations had large navies which were continually fighting, and which were continually renewed. The vessels of the Numbfudgeons were invariably destroyed, and as they were usually burned up, with a prodigious slaughter of their crews and fighting men, this part of the play was performed at night, when miniature crafts, built of shingles, and rigged with birch bark, were set on fire and allowed to consume amid the shouts and cheers of the Pedan generals, who were also admirals.

It was all on account of a list of the Pedan navy falling into the hands of Sam Perkins that the secret of the kingdom of Pedan was allowed to get to the other members of the Fairport Nine. Sam, prowling through Ned Martin's base-ball records, one day, found a sheet of paper headed "List of the Pedan Navy."

"Why, what's this?" he cried, in great amazement, reading the names of the *Ajax*, the *Agamemnon*, the *Minos*, the *Rhadamanthus*, the *Bellona*, and other strange craft. "Is this a new navy that you fellers are building to float in the back cove? Give me a look at it, Ned."

Ned, not without some shamefacedness, as his cherished dream was not easily made understood by another, said, "Well, you see, Sam, we fellows are making believe that there is a kingdom of Pedan, and we are making believe (that is, Billy, Sam Black, and I are) that we are in command of the forces of the King of Pedan, and we go to war with the Numbfudgeons— "

"The what!" shouted Sam. "The Numb— well, I never!" and Sam paused in speechless amazement at the audacity of the imaginary epic which the three boys were engaged in acting.

But Sam's active fancy was tickled with the notion of a party of boys engaged in acting out, every day or two, the battles, sieges, and manœuvres of contending armies. His naturally belligerent disposition was akin to the dreamy delusion which had amused the other boys. In a short time he made himself so thoroughly the master of the situation that he not only understood it, but he invented many new combinations, and was shortly chosen general-in-chief—at least, he was made general-in-chief, though how it was done, nobody could exactly tell. Under his skilful management, the army of the King of Pedan was reorganized. More grumgrudgeons were provided, and the slaughter of the Numbfudgeons was something tremendous. In the words of the General-in-chief, in one of his frequent imaginary bulletins to the people of Pedan, who were represented by a pile of broken lumber behind the barn, "The craven ranks of the enemy had been compelled to bite the dust, and the victorious eagles of the kingdom of Pedan had flapped their wings on every field."

Sam introduced, among other things, the art of fighting wholly imaginary naval battles into the warfare of Pedan and Numbfudgeon. From a poplar tree by the well-house could be obtained a good view of Penobscot Bay; and from this exalted perch it was the duty of Billy Hetherington, as

rear-admiral of the Pedan navy, to descry, or to im-
agine he descried, the fleets of the enemy advancing
up the bay. It was also his duty to shout out the
names of the various hostile vessels, the number
of men which each carried, and her armament.

One day, however, Billy's imagination outran his
discretion. With great enthusiasm, he was shouting, " There comes a fifty-decker, carrying one thousand guns!" and making other astounding an-
nouncements, when, with one bound of his imagination, he screamed, as he gazed upon the shining
surface of the bay, " there comes a five-hundred-
decker!"

A ship with five hundred decks, and five hundred rows of guns, was a little too much for Captain
and Generalissimo Sam, and, catching his breath, he
said with a queer smile, " Why, Billy, a five-hun-
dred-decker would be half a mile high!"

" I don't care," replied Billy, " she's a five-hun-
dred-decker, and here comes a thousand-decker,"
he added, defiantly.

" Oh, well," said Captain Sam, " you're making
this thing ridiculous. Who ever heard of a man-of-
war with a thousand decks and one thousand rows
of guns? Why can't you be reasonable? I never
saw such a chap. Your imagination gets ever so
far ahead of the facts. Call it a hundred-decker,
can't you?"

But Billy was obstinate. It was not worth quarrelling about, as Captain Sam said, and so the fight went on, and when Billy came down from his outlook in the tree, he and his comrades took their " make-believe " ships and sailed into the Numbfudgeon fleet, and, in a few minutes, scattered or sunk the entire force, including the thousand-decker, happily represented by a tall thistle growing in a fence corner. This feat was performed by Billy, whose cries to his crew, joined to those of the other gallant officers of the Pedan navy, so startled Ned Martin's mother, that she laid down her knitting and, gazing over into the orchard, said, " Land sakes alive ! What are those pesky boys doing now, I wonder ? "

Just below the thicket at the bottom of the orchard was a field of grass, and when it was about right for the scythe of the mower, it was a favorite mustering-field for the Numbfudgeons. To the fertile fancy of the boys, the tall ranks of grass, crowned with waving spears of timothy, were the solid phalanxes of the enemy. Here and there a blazing poppy stood for a Numbfudgeon banner, or a stray stalk of yellow dock represented a major-general, at the very least.

But Major Boffin, whose place adjoined that of the Martins, objected to having his tall grass trampled down by the Pedan army, whom he rudely

called "a passel of riotous boys." Several raids
of the Pedan army had been made across the thicket
and into the mowing-field in pursuit of the Numbfudgeons, who retreated with great slaughter, and
made a stand only when they reached the Boffin
estate, where they were mown down in swathes, by
the terrible grumgrudgeons of the Pedan army.

Peletiah Snelgro, who "did chores" about the
Boffin place, heard the complaint of the major,
and, after skulking around on the edge of the field
among the bushes for some time, he discovered
what the martial nine were doing. But it took him a
long time to find out what all this terrific pother was
about. Pel looked on with speechless amazement
from his hiding-place in the bushes, while boy after
boy, led by Captain Sam, came flying through the
thicket, furiously shouting, "Down to the dust with
'em!" "Aha! aha! they fly! The cravens fly!
Long live the King of Pedan, and confusion to his
enemies!" "There falls a regiment with one fell
swoop of my grumgrudgeon!"

Peletiah thought that these boys must be crazy.
"But nine fellers couldn't all get crazy at once," he
reflected. And he whispered to himself, as he
watched the army with wide-open eyes, "Well, this
beats me!"

But Peletiah's bosom was filled with contempt,
when it dawned upon him after awhile, that the

Fairport Nine were only "playing" that they were
an army, and the tall grass and weeds were their
imaginary foes.   With wrath and disgust he went
off and laid his plans.

The very next Saturday afternoon there was another fierce contention in the Martin orchard.   It
began in the back-yard near the wood-pile, where a
considerable force of Numbfudgeons were discovered in ambush.   The enemy was dislodged, chased
through the garden, to the great damage of a patch
of cabbages, many of which were laid low by the
reckless use of grumgrudgeons, as the Pedan army
pursued the flying foe.   The Lob, as usual, came
to grief early.   While trying to avoid a bed of mar-
joram, he fell sprawling into a glass cucumber-
frame.   The crash was terrific, but the Lob escaped with a few scratches and hurried on to join
his comrades, who paused and looked with sore
dismay at the mischief he had wrought.   But Major-General Martin, who was in authority in his
father's garden, cheerily cried, " Never mind, boys,
it's nothing but an old cucumber-frame, and won't
be used again this year."

Reaching the orchard, the imaginary foe made a
bold stand where a few tall stalks of dock were
growing in the shade of the board fence.   These
were quickly razed to the ground by the Pedanites,
and the enemy were driven down the long aisles be-

tween the apple-trees, and over the soft green turf,
flecked with the sunshine that flickered through
the boughs. Out into the open, now shimmering
with summer heat, and into the tangled thicket of
alder, blackberry, and dog-wood, the panic-stricken
Numbfudgeons were supposed to flee.

Shouting, " Down with the craven Numbfudgeons ! " Captain Sam bounded through the brush,
and leaping over the low stone wall, charged upon
the enemy in the tall grass beyond. He was
followed by Ned Martin, Billy Hetherington, Hi
Hatch, and Blackie. Scarcely had they begun to
belabor the tall grass with their grumgrudgeons, a
fresh patch being selected for this occasion, than
they were astonished by a great shout of " Down
with the Pedanties ! " which came from their rear.
In an instant, Pel Snelgro, Dan Morey, Joe Fitts,
Eph Weeks, and Joe Patchen, burst from the under-
brush, where they had been concealed, and fell upon
the gallant army of Pedan in rear.

Somewhat dismayed by this unexpected movement, and possibly a little bit ashamed of being
caught in such boys' play, Captain Sam faltered
for a moment, when he had turned around to face
the foe ; but Ned Martin, not in the least taken off
his guard, apparently, cried in shrill tones, " Down
with the cowardly Numbfudgeons, up guards and
at 'em ! " This was Ned's favorite rallying cry, for

he was a close student of histories of great battles, and when he quoted Wellington's saying at Waterloo, every boy knew that he meant confusion and disaster to the Numbfudgeons.

"We'll teach you fellers to come in here trampling Major Boffin's grass down!" cried Joe Patchen. With that he made a terrible lunge at Ned Martin, and striking his grumgrudgeon, sent it flying through the air, eight or ten feet away, when it fell out of sight in the long grass. Ned, though disarmed, was not at a loss for an expedient, but snatched Sam Black's weapon from his hand, and, before Joe could parry the blow, dealt him a resounding thwack on his hard head.

"Ouch!" bawled Joe, rubbing his skull, "that's no fair play to hit a chap on the sconce. That's not the way the Numbfudgeons fight."

"That's the way the Pedan army fight, any way," retorted Ned, "and if you don't like it, you had better get out of this pretty quick."

In the meantime, Blackie, who had been much annoyed by the loss of his grumgrudgeon, took advantage of Joe's temporary discomfiture, and while that worthy was rubbing his smarting scalp, he stole up behind him, and snatched Joe's cudgel from his loose grasp. Seeing this, Joe turned upon him fiercely, but Blackie was too quick for him, and Billy Hetherington, seeing the fracas at this point,

ran, and putting his grumgrudgeon between Joe's
legs, tripped him so that he fell heavily in the
grass. Instantly two or three boys were on his
back and it was declared that Joe was fairly taken
prisoner.

The contest waged all over the field, the Pedanites, or Fairport Nine holding their own pretty
well, but being driven hither and yonder, as the
tide of victory was with them or with the Numbfudgeons, otherwise White Bears. It must be
admitted that the slaughter of the Numbfudgeons
was very great, if it was considered that only the
long grass represented the enemy. The mowing
field was completely trodden down by the flying
feet of the two armies, who raged to and fro, each
valiant soldier intent on dealing as many hard
knocks on his foeman's shins as possible.

The Pedanites had been driven well out into the
centre of the field, which would really have been
in the heart of the enemy's country, when Major
Boffin, hearing the racket, as he came jogging along
the road, which skirted the upper edge of his field,
on horseback, stood in his stirrups and gazed upon
the scene. The major beheld two squads of boys
struggling in the midst of his sacred mowing field,
and trampling down the long grass in every direction. There were shouting, strange discordant
cries, boys pommelling each other, and bawling

7

something about the King of Pedan, whoever he
might be, and Numb—something or other, with
other words which the good major remembered
were in his reading-books when he was a lad.

"Now this beats all natur'!" said the major, as,
dismounting from his horse, he climbed the stone
wall, and viewed with grief and rage the destruc-
tion of his hay crop. "And if there isn't that
lazy, good-for-nothing Pel in the midst, a layin'
about him for dear life, and a yellin' louder'n any
on 'em. Oh, I'll baste him!" Then raising his
voice, he shouted, "Get out o' that long grass, you
rascals!"

At the sound of Major Boffin's voice, the battle
was instantly suspended. The boys looked at the
major for an instant with speechless terror, for he
was one of the selectmen, and to be one of the
selectmen was to be one of the governors of the
town—a terror to evil-doers.

The contending armies of Pedanites and Numbfudgeons looked ruefully at each other for an instant, then at the trampled grass about them, and
it suddenly dawned on them, for the first time, that
they had been doing a great deal of mischief, un-
thinkingly. Then nearly every boy turned and
fled, rushing through the tall grass in all directions.
Some dropped on their faces in the tall grass, and
so wriggled their way out of sight. Others lay flat

in the fragrant grass and with beating hearts waited
to see what would come next.

Almost everybody had vanished out of sight,
when the angry major, fastening his horse to the
fence, strode down to where Billy Hetherington,
Blackie, and Ned Martin stood together to face the
storm.

"What in time hev you been doin' here, boys?
Why I should think that you were a pack of crazy
critters, by your goin's-on, layin' about you, and
bawlin' and takin' on like mad. And just look at
that grass! My! what a sight!" and the major's
anger rose.

"We didn't mean to, Major!" said Ned,
meekly.

"Didn't mean to!" retorted the major, with
something very like a snort. "Didn't mean to!
Why what were you in here for, a-trampin' down
my tall grass? Didn't you know that this was
trespass, and I might have you up before the
selectmen for it? Didn't mean to! Just like boys,
for all the world."

"Well, you see, Major," broke in Billy Hetherington, "we were playing—making believe that
we were fighting an enemy—"

"Hey, British? I spose," demanded the major,
sarcastically.

"No, sir ; we were making believe that we were fighting an imaginary enemy, the—the—Numb-fudgeons."

"The Numb—well, I never!" exclaimed the major, his grim face relaxing a little at the oddity of the conceit. "So you make believe, as you call it, that those other boys, the White Bears, I think they call themselves, were Numb—what's-its-name ? —and you chose my mowing-field for a battle-ground. Well, now, I like that, especially because it's trespass."

"No, sir !" exclaimed Ned, "we were not mak-ing believe that the White Bears were the—the- . Numbfudgeons, but that the tall grass was, and we were beating it down (just a little) round the edges with our grum—our sticks, when some of the White Bear fellers, led on by Peletiah Snelgro, took us in the rear, and they drove us out into the middle of the field." And Ned gazed about him ruefully at the mischief they had wrought.

"What'll have to be done with you boys? I guess you'll have to be prosecuted for trespass, won't ye ? And I'll have to tell your folks, and some of you will get an awful thrashing at home, I'll be bound."

"We are real sorry, Major Boffin," said Billy, sorely dismayed at the prospect of having to face

the selectmen in council, as well as grief and in-
dignation at home. " We are really sorry, and we
didn't intend any harm. We got to fighting with
the Numb—I mean scuffling with the other fellows,
before we thought. It was heedlessness, and I 'll
never do so again."

" Are you sorry because you have done the mischief, or sorry because you are caught at it ? " demanded the major.

" Oh, we might have got away, just as the other
fellows did," cried Blackie, " but we stayed to face
the music, and I 'm sorry because I did so much
damage. I never thought what I was about until
it was all over."

" Now, that 's all right," said Major Boffin heartily.
" It 's all right, and spoken man-fashion. But I don't
think you other two chaps think as this little black
feller does. Now do ye? Own up."

Ned and Billy very humbly and honestly confessed that they were wrong, and that they were
sorry for what they had done. Billy, for his part,
said, that if he had not been caught he would have
" owned up," if he had been questioned about
it.

" That 's all I want," said the major. " If you
are really sorry, and say so, I 'll call it square.
Now, boys, you go right home and tell your folks

what you have done, and tell them that I have let you off because you are sorry for it."

The boys, much humbled, but relieved of mind, walked quietly homeward. Then the major's face darkened, and he growled, " Now, where 's that good-for-nothing Pel ? "

CHAPTER XII.

A WHITE BEAR IN TROUBLE.

PELETIAH was so astonished and scared by the turn which affairs had taken, that he fled over the fields, across Windmill Hill, and into the burying-ground, before he stopped. The village burying-ground, which is on a bleak hill overlooking Fairport and the harbor, is never a very cheerful-looking place. But when Pel, breathless with running, dropped down behind a whitewashed fence, and lay in the cool and fragrant grass, he felt that here, at least, he was secure. He dreaded the vengeance of the Fairport Nine, and, as his eyes wandered over the slate-colored and white gravestones, so ghastly in the bright summer sunlight, he murmured to himself, "Hokey! how those fellers will whale me if they ever catch me away from the rest of the chaps."

"But they shan't catch me," he added, reflectively. "I'll manage to keep around with Dan Morey and Joe Fitts. They can lick Ned Martin, and that stuck-up Sam Perkins, any day. And I 'll tell the major—— " But, at the thought of the major and his dreadful vengeance, Pel's heart stood still. For, after all, he had not so much to dread the Fairports, as his employer, into whose mowing-field he had brought a party of boys and had done infinite mischief. Peletiah's father lived " off the Neck," two or three miles away. The boy did not dare go home to him without some kind of an explanation, much less did he dare to go back to the major's house, where he belonged, as Major Boffin kept a birch rod over the mantel-shelf, with the taste of which Peletiah was very familiar.

As the boy, feeling very miserable and guilty, turned over in his mind the various troubles before him, he was suddenly startled by something which fell over the fence, and on his back, as he lay flat on his stomach, nibbling at the white clover tops, looking at the headstones, and wondering what he should do next. With a howl of terror, Peletiah struggled out from under the object, which seemed to be alive and kicking. Sitting up on end he beheld the familiar face of little Sam Murch.

" Why, what do ye want to scare a feller right out of his wits for, I 'd like to know ? Comin' right down on a feller's back when he 's layin' off in the grass and enjoyin' himself. Don't ye know nothin' scarcely ? My ! how you hurt my head with your bony knees!" And Pel rubbed his red head by way of emphasis.

"Why," cried Sam, "how did I know you were hiding behind the fence? I was going down to Hatch's Cove to fish for cunners. There's my basket, see? It flew right out in the middle of that lot when I fell on you," and Sam went to pick up his fugitive basket.

"What are you doing here, Pel, hiding behind the fence, all alone by yourself, I'd like to know?" asked Sam, lazily throwing himself down on the turf.

"None of your business," cried Peletiah roughly; "can't a feller lay down in the shade of a pleasant day, and think things over? But, I say, if you're goin' fishin' I'll go along; I've got a first-rate line in my pocket, and I know a place down there on Hatch's Point, where we can cut a mighty nice pole."

Anything, Pel thought to himself, was better than worrying about his present troubles and the necessity of getting home, some way, when night came. Going fishing was an easy way out of the present difficulty.

Just then, hearing the sound of voices on the other side of the fence, Pel applied his eye to a knot-hole, and in great alarm cried, "Here come the Fairports! Run, run for your life!" and seiz-

7*

ing the basket, he fled like a deer, dodging among
the headstones and even jumping over the mossy
graves, which, as every boy knows, is sure to bring
bad luck.

Looking over the fence, Sam saw Billy Hetherington and Sam Black climbing the little hill below.
They hailed him cheerily, and seeing Pel flying over
the burying-ground, they sarcastically cried, "'Rah
for the King of Pedan! 'rah!"

"What's the matter with Pel Snelgro, Sammy?"
said Billy Hetherington.

"I can't guess," replied Sam, "he and I were
talking of going a-fishing, when he saw you coming
up the hill, and then he bawled, 'Here come the
Fairports,' and away he scud like a quarter-horse.
And he's got my basket," added Sam, "and Joe's
best fishing line is in it."

"Oh, well," explained Blackie, "we were not
chasing Pel. He thought we were after him,
because he got us into trouble down in the major's
mowing field. He got a lot of White Bears in
there and we had a scrimmage, and while we were
at it, and trampling the grass all down, the major
came in and caught us, and then Pel and the other
chaps ran off."

"My," said Sam, with his eyes distended wide,
"didn't you catch it, though. Who else did he
lick besides you two fellers?"

"No, we told him we were sorry," said Billy, "and he said if we were sorry, it was all right, though I own up I was plaguy scared for awhile. I thought we were going before the selectmen for sure."

"If we had n't said we were sorry because we had done the mischief, not because we were caught," explained Blackie, "we certainly would not have got off so easy."

"Now you go along and find Pel, and tell him that Blackie and I are not hunting him. Major Boffin will fix him when he goes home with his cows to-night, that 's all."

"And tell him," added Billy, "that he need n't have run, a guilty conscience needs no accuser."

"Yes," said Blackie, "and tell him, too, that the wicked flee when nobody 's chasing him. That will hit him harder."

"Well, give it to him straight then, Sammy," said Billy, good-naturedly. "It 's 'The wicked flee when none pursueth.' Now get yourself hence."

"The wicked flea ?" queried Sam.

"Oh, get thee gone," cried Blackie. And Sammy got himself thence ; but coming to the stone wall which separated the burying-ground from Hatch's apple orchard, he suddenly bethought himself:

" Now what did those fellows want to get rid of
me for ? I 'll just bet they were going a-money-
digging down in Hatch's pasture," and fired by
this tardy reflection, Sam stood upon the wall and
gazed anxiously after the two boys, but they had
disappeared in the spruce thicket.

Sam bent his steps toward the rocky shore of
the cove, scolding himself as he went for not
having discovered that the other boys wanted to
" get rid of him " before they had got rid of him ;
but he was speedily joined by Pel, who, from his concealment in the thicket, saw him approaching alone.

" Where 's those other chaps ? " demanded Pel.

" Don't know," replied Sam, sulkily, " what did
you run off so for ? "

" Oh, never you mind, Sammy," said Peletiah,
persuasively, " let 's get down to the cove before
the tide turns. It 's a first-rate day for fishin'."
And he dashed into the thicket, closely followed
by Sam, who soon forgot Billy, Blackie, and their
possible projects of money-digging.

" I know what you ran away for," said Sam, as
scrambling over the rail fence, the two boys were
at the edge of the cove.

" Well, I don't care if you do," retorted Pel.
" Fishing is the business just now, so you may
shut up your clamshell about Major Boffin and
his tall grass."

It was high water and there was a good prospect
for catching a nice mess of fish from the rocks.
There was some dispute as to who should first hold
the line, for they found that they had but one hook
between them, and that was Sam's, or, rather, his
brother Joe's. But Peletiah, who was in the habit
of having his own way with boys smaller than himself, baited the hook with great care, and dropping
it into the pool said, "You let me catch the first
fish, Sammy, my boy, and I 'll let you catch the
next two. That 's fair, I 'm sure."

"A bite! a bite!" he roared, and drew the
struggling little fish carefully to the surface, playing
along the top of the water.

Just then Major Boffin, who was on his way off
the Neck, to tell Mr. Snelgro that he might keep
Peletiah when he returned home, as he believed he
would that night, cast his eye along the shore of
the cove, and saw the two boys sitting on the
rocks, fishing.

"That 's that young jackanapes, I 'll be bound,"
muttered the major, looking intently over the top
of his spectacles. "It is, I 'm dead sure of it."

So saying, the major rode softly back to the pasture gate, which he pushed open, and then made
his way to the fence by the shore, where, leaving
his horse tied, he clambered over, being hid by a
lump of maples.

"He's caught! he's caught!" cried Pel in great glee, as he drew the fish in shore.

"Yes, and you're caught too," echoed a grim and dreadful voice behind him. And Pel, turning his head, saw Major Boffin, apparently fifteen feet high, standing directly behind him. The major's appearance was dreadful, and in his hand he held a birch-rod, newly cut.

Sam, with the natural instinct of a small boy, rolled himself hastily out of the way, without waiting to hear what the major had to say. He knew well enough what was coming, and when Major Boffin sternly said to the blubbering Peletiah, "What do you mean by bringing in a lot of boys to trample down my tall grass?" Sam was not surprised that his comrade had no answer. Nor was he at all astonished when the angry major let fall a couple of smart blows on the shrinking legs of Peletiah.

"Oh, oh," shrieked the lad, almost before he was hurt, "I did n't mean to!"

"Well, what did you do it for? You knew I had forbidden you to go into the field yourself, and yet you not only went in there, but brought in a whole passel of other boys with you." And the old gentleman cut Pel sharply about the legs once more.

"I wanted to drive out the Fairports, who were

coming in there to raise the mischief," bawled poor
Pel, at his wits' end for an answer which would
satisfy his employer. The old man fairly laughed
at this childish excuse, and laid on with the switch
until he thought that the lad was sufficiently pun-
ished; then, releasing his grasp on Peletiah's collar,
he told him to go home to his father and say to
him that he had finished his work with Major Boffin.

When the squire had climbed over the fence,
mounted his horse, and slowly ridden away, Peletiah, who had sullenly watched him, said, "Well,
you won't catch me doing any more favors for old
Boffin after this, now you just better believe."

Sam agreed that this was not very likely, as the
major had just sent him home to his father. "And
besides," added Sam, "I don't see how you tried
to do him any favor this time. You were more in
favor of driving out the Fairports than you were
of helping Major Boffin; now, were n't you, Pel?
Own up that you were."

It was useless for Pel to attempt to answer this,
but he felt himself an injured and much-abused
boy, for all that. He could not see how his original intentions had been misunderstood. He had
certainly meant well.

As the two boys climbed back the hill, after
catching a few more fish, they met Billy Hethering-

ton and Blackie, who, instead of money-digging,
had been out to look at a rabbit-trap which they
had set in the thicket, and from which they had
taken a pretty little gray fellow, with bright eyes
and soft fur. Both boys speedily forgot all about
their encounter with the major while admiring
the beautiful creature which nestled in Blackie's
bosom, as if it was not afraid of him, but of the
others.

" See," exclaimed Billy, admiringly, " that rab-
bit knows that Blackie will not hurt him. No
other fellow could handle a wild thing like that.
But what 's the matter with your eyes, Pel, you
look as if you 'd been crying. Have you and
Sammy been fighting ? "

Peletiah acknowledged, casting down his eyes,
and digging his toes into the grass, in an embar-
rassed way, that he had had a whipping from Major
Boffin.

" Why, what was that for ? " demanded Blackie.
" I suppose you deserved it for something ; you
most always are up to some sort of mischief."

" I don't think he deserved all he got, though,"
replied Sammy, manfully. " He got the White
Bears into the major's field, to keep you fellows
from trampling down the grass ; and so the whole
party of you did an awful lot of mischief—so the
major says—and that 's why he gave such a wallop-

ing to Pel, just now. My! but did n't he catch it.
Roll up your trousers, Pel, and show 'em where
he welted you with the birch."

This Peletiah refused to do, and he added that if
he was in Sam's place, he would not crow over a
fellow who had had a whipping that he did not
deserve. The lad was very much cast down—as
what boy would not be?—at this discussion of his
mishaps.

"Why did n't you tell him you were sorry
because you had done the mischief, not because
you had been found out?" demanded Blackie, a
sudden light breaking in on him. "That's what
we did, and he let us off."

"He let you off just for saying that?" asked
Pel, in great amazement.

"Yes, he did," answered Billy, "and when we
said it was because we had done the mischief, not
because we were caught, he seemed real pleased,
and said he would not make any complaint about
us."

"Well! I never!" said Pel, and he could not
understand this new view of the major's character.

Just then, Billy, winking at Blackie, seized poor
Pel by the shoulders, and, throwing himself on
him, cried, "Now, I 've got you! you are the fellow that got us into trouble by bringing the White
Bears down on us, and then bringing the major

down on them. Now you'll have to catch it from the Fairports."

"Let me up! let me up, I say!" bawled Pele-tiah, struggling to be free. But Billy, who was the heavier boy of the two, calmly sat astride of the prostrate body of the lad, and declared that he would not let him get up until he acknowledged that he had done wrong, and that he was sorry for it.

"I am sorry," howled Pel, in a muffled voice, his face buried in the grass. "I tell you I am ever so sorry; and I know you can lick me; so let me up."

"No," said Billy, with another prodigious wink at the other two boys. "No, I shall not let you up until you say that you are sorry for having got us into trouble, not that I have caught you."

"I am sorry both ways," said poor Pel. "Sorry that I got you into trouble, and sorry that you caught me. So now!"

This explanation satisfied Billy, who, with a laugh, let Pel get up again. That worthy youth, flushed and angry at his rough treatment, stood off from the group a little distance, and saying, "I'll get my big brother Ike to give you a thrashing, some day, you Bill Hetherington," fled down the hill and disappeared among the bushes.

As the boys went thoughtfully homewards, puz-zling over the moral lessons of the afternoon, Billy said, "After all, boys, I don't think that I did Pel Snelgro one bit of good. He went off mad."

CHAPTER XIII.

A YARN FROM GLOUCESTER.

In October, Jake Coombs came back from his fishing voyage. It had been a fortunate venture, and the appearance of the trim little schooner, the *Diana*, as she sailed up the harbor, laden deeply, showed that she had a full fare of fish. Jake was, accordingly, "mighty cranky," as the boys said; for in those days, fishermen on the Banks were paid in proportion to the catch. The very next day after the arrival of the *Diana*, as Blackie was lounging in the window of the house on stilts which overlooked the harbor, Jake, slouching along the beach below, laden with fishing tackle, made a speaking trumpet of his hand and bawled:

"Say, Blackie, ahoy!"

Sam, in the same humor, shouted back, "Ahoy yourself! What luck!"

Jake, having arrived opposite the house, made answer, "Now, if you fellows want to try another

game with the White Bears, before the fall rain sets
in, we are ready for you."

"We are always ready for the White Bears, and
you know it, Jake," was Blackie's reply. "But
you need n't think that, just because you had a
good shake on your lay of the *Diana's* catch, you
are agoing to carry all before you."

"Ha! ha!" laughed Jake, "you Fairports are
not smart enough to take that pennant from the
White Bears, I calculate, and we are willing to give
you another try at it just for luck. I 've got something I want to tell you, Blackie; come down on
the wharf, just half a minute."

Johnson's Wharf, where the *Diana* lay moored,
was a sleepy and quiet place. It was dotted over
with rows of empty sugar hogsheads, from which
the boys had long since scraped all the loose sugar
left sticking to the fragrant staves. Piles of rusty
chain-cables lay against the weather-beaten store-
house, and two or three huge anchors sunned themselves at the head of the wharf. Nailed against the
gable of the store-house, and looking steadily sea-
ward, was the figure-head of the old ship *Arethusa*,
a once-white nymph, very spare in the face and
very full in the bosom, with a broken nose, and an
unseemly daub of tar on her neck, the wanton gift
of some boy. It was a delightful old spot,
full of associations of the sea, and redolent of

tar and sailor's yarns.   Here, on sunny days, the
wandering mariner sat on an anchor-stock and
told to open-eyed and open-eared boys the most astounding tales of moving accidents and hair-breadth
'scapes upon the raging main, and of strange
sights in foreign parts.   And here, sheltered from
the October wind, Jake and Sam sat down in the
sun.

"When we were on the Banks," began Jake,
confidentially, "I found a feller on board a Glo'-
ster schooner—she was a pink-built schooner, with
a big jib and painted red—and he could spin yarns
just everlastingly.   He comes aboard of the *Diana*,
one Sunday, while we was a-layin' off and on, and
me and him got to talkin' about baseball.   It
'pears that he was the pitcher of the Cape Ann
Nine, down to Rockport; but that's neither here
nor there.   What I was comin' at is how we
got to talkin' baseball, and that's about how it
was."

"And you let on and bragged how you and the
rest of the White Bears had whipped the Fairport
Nine, I suppose?   Hey, Jake?"

"Well, Sammy, I did n't throw away no chance
to say a good word for the White Bears; that
would n't be in natur', now would it, Sammy?"
Jake was very friendly, although he had had a
fare from the Banks.   At least, Blackie thought

"But, as I was sayin'," continued   ke, " he was a yarn-spinner, he was; a yarn-spinner from Yarn-spinnersville, as old Keeler would say.   One day, I was tellin' him about how smart you was in the left field, and how you knew more than most white boys, 'specially about things that run in the woods and swim in the sea, and he ups and says, sez he, ' Well, now, if that boy's father is the one that run away from South America in the old brig *Draco*, years and years ago, he must be a mighty old man by this.'   And I said he was."

" He's only sixty-odd," interrupted Sam.

" Oh, sho," replied Jake, " he don't know how old he is.   Nobody ever knows how old a nigger is, 'specially a nigger who has been into slavery."

" Now, don't go off mad," he added, seeing Blackie making an impatient movement, " I ain't half through my yarn yet, so stow your jaw-tackle and hear the rest of it. ' It's mighty curious.   Says the Glo'ster man to me, says he, ' I know all about old Tumble, as you call him.   My gran'ther sailed with Captain Whitney out of Lincolnville, ever so many years ago, and between you and me, he wa' n't too 　d to dicker in the slave-trade once in a while.   Mind,' says this Glo'ster chap, ' I don't say that he was in the slave-trade regular, but he vas n't above taking a dash at it, once in a while.

when the molasses business was dull. He was in
the Trinidad trade, my gran'ther was, and he had
dealings with a skipper that they called Black
Stover, who sailed out of Fairport. This Black
Stover traded all along the Spanish Main, sellin'
slaves from the Gold Coast, as far up north as Oldport, Rhode Island, and as far south as the River
Plate."

"It's a good story, Jake," broke in Blackie,
"but I don't see what it has got to do with
me."

"Hold hard, youngster ; I 'll tell you what it has
got to do with you. This Glo'ster chap he sez to
me, sez he, 'Black Stover, he told my gran'ther
that he brung a likely young nigger from the Congo
to Rio, and that he sold him there and that he
afterward saw him on Spruce Island, in Penobscot
Bay, and that he was called Black. And my gran'-
ther, who is dead and gone since I was forty-three,
said he saw that identical nigger in Fairport, when
he was there, foremost hand on *The Chariot of
Fame*, Captain Whitney, of Lincolnville.' Leastways, that 's what the Glo'ster man told me," and
Jake paused.

Sam laughed loud and long. "Seems like it
tickled you, Blackie," said the young fisherman
from the banks, a little nettled. "Seems as if
it tickled you, though it beats me why it should."

" Well, I was laughing to think that you should be such a fool as to think that anybody would believe such a tough yarn as that."

." I don't care ; there 's the story. All of the fellers in our crew will tell you the same thing. Most of 'em heard it. Jim Snowman, Si Booden, and Steve Morey, I know heard that Glo'ster man tell that story. He said that he remembered his gran'ther very well, and that he used to tell his goings-on all over the world to everybody that would listen to him ; and that his gran'ther actilly believed that one of the slaves that the Black Stover fetched from the Congo Coast to South America afterward escaped to the coast of Maine, the very country that the Black Stover came from ; so now."

Blackie did not feel very happy as he walked slowly up the wharf, turning over in his mind the tale he had just heard. And he was not at all cheered by Jake's shout after him to " go and have it out with the Black Stover's granddaughter, 'Squire Hetherington's wife."

When he reached home, Sam lost no time in solving his doubts. " Tell me, dad," he said to his father, " do you know the name of the captain of the ship that brought you from Africa to Rio ? "

The old man started, and then, recovering himself, said gently, " it war n't no ship, Sammy, it was a brig,—a square-rigged brig. I was too young

8

to know much about ships and vessels, but I know now that she was a square-rigged brig, for I remember just how she looked."

Sam stood too much in awe of his father to show the impatience which he felt at this evasion, and, stifling it as well as he could, he persisted: " Well, what was the name of the captain of the square-rigged brig that brought you over from Africa ? "

" Well, my son, that was a mighty long while ago. Reely, I disremember. Mebbe it was Brown. You remember Captain Brown, Sammy ; he that was lost in the *Two Brothers*. Dear ! dear ! he was a nice man, was Captain Brown ; and he could splice a five-inch hawser better 'n any man I ever see. 'Pears to me that all the smartest men die first ; hey, Sammy ? "

" Well," said Sam, " I saw Jake Coombs, to-day," and he said that when he was on the Banks, this voyage, a Gloucester man came aboard the *Diana* and told him a long yarn about his grandfather who sailed out of Lincolnville, ever so many years ago, and who knew Captain Stover, and that he, whom they call the Black Stover, you know, commanded a slave-trader, on the sly, as it were, and that you came over on his vessel, a square-rigged brig, say from Africa to Rio. Now, what do you think of that for a yarn, dad ? "

"I don't believe a word of it, Sammy!" replied the old man, with great emphasis.

"But Jake says that his grandfather saw you here, long ago, when he was in here on *The Chariot of Fame*," insisted Blackie. "And he says that he knew you because of your name, and that he was sure of your being the same man that the Black Stover brought over from the Congo river?"

"And this Glo'ster man's grandfather knows that I, who was a slip of a boy when the Black Stover brought me over (now, mind, I don't say that he did bring me over, Sammy) was the same man that he saw when *The Chariot of Fame* came in here with that cargo of Cadiz salt, the year that the monument was built on Grindle's Ledge? Why, I remember it just as if it was yesterday, the year that that monument was built! And he says I was the same man? Oh, sho! How folks do talk! It's nothing to be ashamed of. But it's a shame to be a-tellin' that 'Squire Hetherington's wife's father was ever in the slave trade. It's a wicked, wicked thing, so it is, Sammy."

"But the Glo'ster man said so," replied Sam, rather sadly.

"Perhaps the Glo'ster man lied," said the old negro, with a cunning smile.

Sam brightened up and said, "Perhaps the Glo'ster man's gran'ther lied."

" I should n't wonder the least mite if he did."
And this was all that old Tumble could ever be induced to say about the yarn which had been spun
at sea by the man from Glo'ster.

CHAPTER XIV.

THE LAST GREAT MATCH.

IF the town of Fairport had not been speedily stirred up by the news that there was to be a grand final game between the two Nines, it is likely that this revival of the old scandals of the Black Stover's slave-trading pursuits would have caused much talk. As it was, a few ancient ladies who took their tea and their gossip together, whispered to each other that it was "dreffle cu'rous that that old sin would keep a-comin' up to disturb the Hetheringtons; and they so stuck-up and set in their ways, too, only Mis' Hetherington was n't in the least mite proud; but there was the 'Squire, who walked down Main street as if the earth was too mean for him to walk on." But they never got any farther than this. And the younger portion of the population were in a fever over the intelligence that the two Nines would soon play a final match game for the championship.

During the summer, several "scrub" games had

been played by the Fairports, who had supplied the place of the absent Jo Murch by placing George Bridges at first base. Their opponents were usually made up from such members of the White Bears as happened to be at home and at leisure ; and that was not many. Jo Mun·h had not shown himself at any base-ball game, except to sit sullenly on the outside of the field and watch the play, making rough criticism on all that went on. But when it was noised abroad that the Fairports were to play the White Bears once more, Jo commissioned his small brother Sam to hand in his formal resignation to the members of the Nine. It had been all along understood that he was really in with the White Bears, though he had not formally severed his connection with the Fairports.

" Tell Jo," said Captain Sam Perkins, with great severity, " that we should have turned him out if he had not resigned. George Bridges has resigned from the White Bears, and he will have Jo's place. So it is good riddance to bad rubbage, anyhow."

When Jo Murch received this message, he was very angry, and sent word to Captain Sam that he was glad to get out of a Nine that could n't play any better than the Fairports, and that he was tired of being bullied around by a petty tyrant like Sam Perkins. The messenger in this instance was the mild-mannered Sam Murch, and he conveniently forgot to deliver it, and the gallant captain was spared the mortification of this last insult from his rebellious ex-player.

"Now, boys, we must brace up the Nine for the grand combat," said Captain Sam. "If we lick them this time, it will be a big feather in our caps, for they have got one of our best basemen, and we shall have no other chance to play for the pennant until next summer.

Billy Hetherington and Blackie were in favor of recasting the Nine, with the understanding that the Lob should remain at the post of catcher, and that George Bridges, when elected, as he was sure to be, should be put in Jo Murch's old place at first base. To this the rest of the Nine agreed, and, after much discussion, the captain took Hi Hatch's place at second base, Hi going to short-stop, the station formerly held by Captain Sam. Bill Watson and Billy Hetherington changed stations, "Chunky" going to centre field, and Billy to the right field.

The news of this reorganization of the Fairport Nine spread through the town like wild-fire. It was the talk of all the boys and girls; and Jake Coombs, who had become the leader of the White Bears, sitting on the end of Johnson's Wharf, with his big boots dangling over the tide, solemnly advised Captain Sam Booden to do the same thing with the White Bears, if he did not want to "be got away with everlastingly." Booden agreed to this, though with some reluctance. He was jealous of Jake's rising leadership in the Nine. Jake had already had two fights since he returned from the Banks, and he had come off victorious in each.

Jo Murch had been taken into the White Bears, the members sitting on the bottom of old Getchell's boat, which was lying on the beach below the house on stilts. So, by a solemn vote of the Nine, he was put into the station vacated by George Bridges at second base. Captain Sam Booden then took the first base. Dan Morey went to short stop, and "Nosey" went to centre field, while Joe Fitts, who had been the centre-fielder, took Dan Morey's station at left field. It was a complete reorganization. When Captain Sam Perkins heard of it, he laughed and said the White Bears were getting scared. But it was acknowledged by all the boys that the White Bears had strengthened themselves by these changes. This is the way the great match was played :

THE FAIRPORT NINE.

Pitcher—NED MARTIN.
Catcher—JOHN HALE, " The Lob."
First Base—GEORGE BRIDGES.
Second Base—CAPTAIN SAM PERKINS.
Third Base—JAMES PAT ADAMS.

Short Stop—Hi Hatch.
Left Field—Sam Black, "Blackie."
Centre Feld—Bill Watson, "Chunky."
Right Field—Billy Hetherington.

THE WHITE BEARS.

Pitcher—Jake Coombs.
Catcher—Eph Weeks.
First Base—Captain Sam Booden.
Second Base—Jo Murch.
Third Base—Joe Patchen.
Short Stop—Dan Morey.
Left Field—Joe Fitts.
Centre Field—Eph Mullett, "Nosey."
Right Field—Peletiah Snelgro.

The bright blue October sky gave promise of a fine day when the two Nines and their friends assembled in the old fort, once more to try their skill with each other. The air was a little chilly for the girls, who were prettily grouped together on the ramparts, now brown and sear with the frosts of autumn ; but Sarah Judkins, with her customary superior air, said that she could keep warm by merely looking at the exercise of the players.

"And as for me," said Alice Martin, shaking her yellow curls, "I shall be in a fever until I see those horrid White Bears so awfully whipped that they will never dare to say ' base-ball ' again as

8*

long as they live. Just look at that horrid Jake Coombs, now, strutting around as if he owned the whole fort!"

"The stuck-up thing!" said Comfort Stanley, who overheard this remark. But Comfort Stanley referred to Alice, and not to Jake, for whom she entertained a secret admiration. Comfort was a daughter of one of the White Bear families, as that portion of the population of Fairport had come to be called.

The members of the two Nines were too much engrossed in the vast interests which they had now at stake to pay the slightest attention to the light gossip and chatter which reached them faintly from the bright ranks of their girl admirers on the sides of the ramparts. With grave and even anxious face, Sam Perkins cried "Heads!" as the copper cent went up into the air. He lost the toss, and the White Bears, with an elation which they did not try to hide, chose to take the field first. "We lost the toss and we lost the game, last time," whispered Ned Martin to the Captain. "It's a sign of bad luck, isn't it?" Sam made no reply, but gloomily took his place in the line of fellows waiting for their turn at the bat.

"There's no luck in the game, Sam," cheerily said Mr. Nathan Dunbar, who had consented to act as umpire. "It's good playing, my lad, that's go·

ing to win this game, and the fellows that play best
will carry the pennant back to town, and don't you
forget it." Mr. Dunbar was a philosopher. Sam
felt comforted, and his spirits rose with his temper
when he heard Dan Morey say, as he went to
short-stop, "this is agoing to be a regular walk-
over, boys."

Ned Martin went first to the bat. He made a
terrific strike at the first ball pitched, which was
exactly where he wanted it. He hit the ball, but
it struck foul and was caught by Captain Sam
Booden, who played first base for the first time,
and whose dexterity was applauded vigorously by
Comfort Stanley, and her friends on the fort. Ned
having been called out by the umpire, retired, and
his place was taken by The Lob, who was soon retired, going out on strikes. Next came Hi Hatch,
and when he took up the bat a general murmur of
approval ran over the spectators. Hiram was a
prime favorite. He made a capital hit, knocking
the ball over Dan Morey's head at short-stop. Hi
was the first man who had reached the first base,
and as soon as Jake Coombs had pitched the ball to
George Bridges, who now took up the bat for the
Fairports, Hi started for second base and safely
reached it. But when he next attempted to run to
third base, Joe Fitts, in some mysterious manner,
got in from left field, and Eph Weeks, the catcher,

threw him the ball, and Hi was caught between the
bases and so put out. Thus ended the first half
of the first inning.

"They 're blanked! they 're blanked!" cried
Hannah Kench, one of the friends of the White
Bears. Sarah Judkins looked calmly over Hannah's
head, and said to her comrades that she thought
that there were more ill-mannered people this year
than usual.

There was exultation when the White Bears now
went to the bat, the redoubtable Jake Coombs being the first striker. He led off with a safe base
hit, Eph Weeks being next after him. Eph struck
the first ball pitched, to Hi Hatch at short stop. Hi
handled it with lightning rapidity to Sam Perkins,
at second base, and he in turn sent it flying to first
base, and both men were put out by the skilful
playing of these two, amidst great applause from
all the spectators. Even the friends of the White
Bears lent a hand to cheer the Fairports.

Thus the Fairports were credited with a very fine
double play, and when their old first base man, Jo
Murch, stood up at the bat, as he came next, a perceptible smile of triumph spread over the faces of
the martial Nine. There were murmurs of disappro-
bation, too, on the slopes of the fort, where some
of the girls recalled Jo's desertion from his company. And when he was disposed of by his ball

bounding right into the catcher's hand, even the champions of the White Bears secretly thought that it served him right. Somehow, Jo had lost caste by his desertion.

The first inning was now completed, both Nines being whitewashed. The second inning opened with Pat Adams at the bat. He knocked a daisy-cutter over to Pel Snelgro, in the right field, so swiftly that it could not be stopped. This was a fine hit, and, with great enthusiasm prevailing, Pat made his second base from it. Sam Perkins followed with a single baser, which advanced Pat Adams to the third base. Sam Black, who was next in order, disappointed his friends, as he "hit Barlow," and was put out at first base, to his own great mortification. The spirits of the Fairports were revived by "Chunky," who, striking wildly and ineffectually at the two first balls, hit the third with a tremendous crack and sent it flying between centre and right fields, thus bringing Pat Adams home, and sending the gallant captain to the second base. Billy Hetherington, coming next to the bat, hit a short ball to Jo Murch at second base, and gave the White Bears a double play and ended the second inning of the Fairports, with one run to their credit.

Again the Bears went to the bat, but with ill-fortune attending them, as their three strikers went in one—two—three order.

"Another blank for the White Bears!" cried
Ned Martin, exultingly, as he came up to the bat.
"It is n't such bad luck to lose the toss, after all;
is it, Sam?" but Ned's elation was soon over. All
three of the strikers went out, as the White Bears
had just gone, on strikes.

There was a solemn hush inside the fort when the
third inning opened with only one run scored.
The crisis was an exciting one. Some terrific batting was done in the last half of this inning by Jake
Coombs, Eph Weeks and Jo Patchen. They succeeded in earning two runs before they were retired; and the fourth inning began with the Fairports at the bat. But they were retired with a
blank, only one base hit being made, and that was
Hi Hatch's. He did not succeed in getting any
further than first base, the three players following
him striking out. The White Bears watched the
field so closely that it was impossible to steal
around, and the Fairports took the field again somewhat down-hearted. Ned Martin, as he went to his
position confided to Blackie his worst fears.

"They think they 've got us," said Ned.

Blackie laughed confidently and made no answer.
But he knew that the score stood 2 to 1 against
them.

The White Bears now went in to end the fourth
inning, with Sam Booden at the bat. He led off

with a fly to the left field, which Blackie caught with one hand, after a long run. Eph Mullett, who came next, made a fine hit over the centre-fielder's head, on which he got his second base. Dan Morey followed with a single base hit which put Eph to third base, and from thence he attempted to steal home; but he was caught between the bases and was put out by " The Lob " after a lively struggle. Joe Fitts coming next to the bat, sent the first ball pitched to Billy Hetherington, in the right field, and Billy held it and thus the inning was ended, the Bears being retired with another blank, to the great delight of some of the girls, Sarah Judkins saying that it was just what might have been expected.

Billy Watson went first to the bat for the Fairports, and, as he took his station, little Sam Watson, who could not suppress his admiration for the martial Nine, shrilly shrieked, " Now give it to 'em, ' Chunky,' " to the great scandal of Captain Sam Perkins, who shouted " Silence in the ranks." This made all the girls laugh, and Jake Coombs, at pitcher's station, satirically said that the captain of the Fairports had not got his sea-legs on yet.

" Chunky " knocked a liner over to centre field, the ball flying directly over the head of Ephraim Mullett. By very hard running, Bill managed to reach the third base, where he paused, quite out of breath. Billy Hetherington followed with a foul fly which he sent straight into the catcher's hands, and then gave way to Ned Martin, who came to the rescue in fine style. Ned made a fine two base hit which brought Watson home amidst great excitement, the score now standing 2 to 2.

Then John Hale, otherwise "The Lob," went out on a fly to Dan Morey at short stop. Hi Hatch hit a grounder to the pitcher and was cut off at first base, which left Ned Martin on the third base, to which he had stolen. In the last half of this inning (the fifth), the White Bears were soon disposed of, Pel Snelgro hitting a fly to Ned Martin, at pitcher, who held it after a great deal of fumbling. The next two strikers, Jake Coombs and Eph Mullett, hit high balls to Pat Adams, at third base, and he closed on them, and umpire Dunbar declared them out.

Even the chattering girls on the ramparts of the fort were hushed as the sixth inning opened with the Fairports at the bat. But it was a short inning. Both sides scored blanks, still leaving the score 2 and 2. The "Lob" opened the next inning for the Fairports. He made a base hit, and Hi Hatch succeeded him with a hit to centre field. Eph let the ball pass him, and the "Lob" got home on his error, and Hiram went to his third base. George Bridges, Pat Adams, and Sam Perkins followed with very weak hits to short stop and second base, but the ball was fumbled each time. The White Bears began to show signs of dismay. Jake Coombs, although the air was cool, was in a state of redness and perspiration wonderful to behold. Before his comrades could recover themselves, the Fairports had made four runs. They then retired in capital spirits.

The flutter of the white handkerchiefs on the fort signalled the triumph they felt at the new turn of affairs in the field. Perhaps the high beating of the proud hearts of the gallant Nine caused them to become a little reckless. The White Bears scored two unearned runs in this inning, on account of errors at short stop, first, and third base, and centre field.

" This will never do, my lads," whispered Captain Sam, between his teeth. " Here we are at the end of the seventh inning, and are only 6 to their 4.

But the eighth inning retrieved the day. Captain Sam's repeated cautions to his fellows were not in vain, and the Fairports, with skilful playing and good running, succeeded in adding 2 more to their score ; their opponents retired without making one run.

Now came the ninth and final inning, with every-thing looking bright for the Fairports. But the White Bears were by no means discouraged.

Jake Coombs, their leading spirit, cheered them by his confident bearing and his rough wit at the expense of their adversaries. Under this stimulus, they went to work with a will. When the Fairports went to the bat for the last time, they did some first-rate batting, but the ball was handled so skilfully, that they found it impossible to gain their first base once, and were retired with a blank. Then the White Bears went to the bat for their last time, the inning being opened by Eph Mullett who made a two-base hit, Dan Morey following him with a single hit, which sent Mullett to third base. Joe Fitts, who next took up the bat, made a splendid hit, sending the ball between centre and left field, and thus brought Ephraim home and Dan Morey to the third base. When Ned Martin delivered the ball for Peletiah Snelgro to strike at, Joe Fitts attempted to run to second base, but the "Lob," catcher, had the ball there before him, and he was cut off by Sam Perkins' fielding it home. This made two men out, two strikes on the third man at the bat ; and the next ball pitched would probably decide the game. Comfort Stanley rose up in great excitement, obscuring the view of several persons behind her, for she was a big girl, whereat Sarah Judkins called her "an ill-mannered old thing." But this was all that was said on the ramparts, where the excitement was intense:

Pel Snelgro at the bat, hit the ball and sent it straight to "Chunky," in centre field. Bill closed on the ball, doubling himself together in his anxiety to keep it. A great sigh of relief was breathed through the ball-field, for the game was won and the Fairports were victorious. A shrill cheer ran along the ramparts of the fort, and Phebe Sawyer, taking her bonnet by the strings, waved it wildly around her head. Then the Fairports gave a loud yell of triumph, and Mr. Dunbar, after a little figuring, mounted a bench and announced the following as the result of the final championship game :

	1	2	3	4	5	6	7	8	9	
The Fairport Nine	0	1	0	0	1	0	4	2	0	—8
The White Bears	0	0	2	0	0	0	2	0	1	—5

Time of game, two hours.
Umpire, Mr. Nathan Dunbar.
Runs earned—Fairport Nine, 3; White Bears, 2.

"Never mind, boys," said Jake Coombs, stoutly, "they had to work hard for it, and we'll get that pennant back, next year ; see if we don't."

"It's not so big as the *William and Sally's* burgee, but it is ours!" cried Blackie, quoting the very words of triumph used by the White Bears when they had captured the pennant, last July. Jake laughed good-humoredly, for he saw the joke, and he was not so mean as to grudge the Fairports their hard-earned victory.

Alice Martin and some of the other girls of the Fairport Nine friends, clustered around Billy Hetherington, who, as the standard-bearer of the martial Nine, was entrusted with the championship pennant.

" It 's just splendid," said Alice, with her blue eyes gleaming, " and I knew we should get the pennant back again."

" We, indeed ! " cried Sarah ; " I 'd like to know what *we* have had to do with it ? "

" Well, I don't care," replied Alice, " everybody that is anybody is awful glad that our Nine have won the victory."

And, as the boys went joyfully down into the town, Billy Hetherington, who lagged behind with the pennant proudly waving over his head, whispered to Blackie, " I don't believe in luck, but I felt it in my bones that the base-ball championship belonged to the Fairport Nine."

.

END.

www.ingramcontent.com/pod-product-compliance
Lightning Source LLC
Chambersburg PA
CBHW030841270326
41928CB00007B/1159